ROMAN CATHOLICISM AND THE BIBLE

ROMAN CATHOLICISM
AND
THE BIBLE

compiled by
OLIVIER BEGUIN
General Secretary of the United Bible Societies

ASSOCIATION PRESS
New York

First published 1963

Published in the U.S.A. by
ASSOCIATION PRESS
291 Broadway New York 7, N.Y.

*Printed in Great Britain by Richard Clay and Company, Ltd.,
Bungay, Suffolk*

CONTENTS

Introduction

THE following document was originally prepared, in response to a request, in the early autumn of 1962 for the information of Bible Society Secretaries. It is a follow-up to a first study (*Bulletin of the United Bible Societies*, No. 34, 1958), which gave a quick historical sketch and some current illustrations of the biblical movement in the Roman Catholic Church. The material, though by no means exhaustive, proved very abundant, while certain of the discussions at the Vatican Council II last autumn served to enhance its significance. Its publication in booklet form was therefore suggested. In preparing the manuscript for the press a few complementary data have been added, particularly the notes relative to the Vatican Council II.

1. The recovery of confidence in the Bible, in the Roman Catholic Church, is growing and spreading. This is the basic fact. The following pages, even when they report on the pressure of the opposition (see Chapter 3, for instance), provide clear evidence of this. Pope John XXIII, right at the beginning of his ministry, stressed the importance of Scripture reading in his sermon on the occasion of his enthronement in the Lateran Church:

> If, therefore, we set great store by all the solicitude of pastoral ministry and if we note its urgency, we feel above all that it is our duty, by continuous action everywhere to arouse enthusiasm for every revelation of the holy Book which is given to light the path of life from childhood to old age.

And ten months later, on the occasion of the 16th Bible Week in Rome, the Pope stated:

> The widespread growth of Bible study today, especially the circulation of new editions of Holy Scripture, adapted to the needs and degree of learning of the various members of the Church, gives rise to the hope that there will be a renewal of Christian life, nourished at the

> very fountain-head of the Revelation. We therefore cannot but encourage every effort which aims at drawing souls nearer to the Bible, the life-giving source of spiritual doctrine.

Again, on January 9, 1963, addressing a large gathering of pilgrims in Rome, Pope John XXIII expressed the same concern, but this time as a direct challenge to the laity, when he asked them:

> Every day you read papers and books, but do you also take time to read the Holy Scriptures?

2. It would be erroneous, however, to assume that the biblical movement has yet reached the masses. Bible reading within the Roman Catholic Church is still far from being current practice and from being encouraged everywhere. The prices and circulation figures of most Roman Catholic editions give more than sufficient evidence of this. The lack of Roman Catholic translations of the Bible is another determinant factor, when it is remembered that the use of Protestant editions without notes and comments is not encouraged or even allowed for ordinary, unprepared members of the Church. But within that general framework the frail plant of the biblical movement goes on thrusting down its roots and gaining in strength. The last two chapters of this book show some of the ways in which this is happening.

3. The first chapters, on the other hand, explore new ground. The concerns for a more live celebration of the Church's liturgy and for deeper religious education rank high in the general preoccupations of a large section of clergy and even among lay people. The deliberations at the Vatican Council II on the Schema on Liturgy showed how widespread and intense is the desire among the Church Fathers for a more pastoral liturgy. And this has a direct bearing on the use of the Bible. Whoever fights for or upholds the necessity of the use of the vernacular in the liturgy is automatically an ally of those who aspire to see the Scriptures made available to Christians in their own language. Whoever wants to help in the training of consecrated, dynamic, responsible, and loyal church members sees the absolute necessity of giving them God's Word in their own tongue. Indirectly,

what happens in the field of liturgy and religious education is determinant for the evolution of the biblical movement.

4. But a new feature is introduced into the whole situation when the concern for the liturgy and for religious education reaches the mission field. Certainly, Roman Catholic missionaries have been more active in translating the Scriptures than is commonly believed, as will be seen from Chapter 4 of this booklet. But the existing translations are far from being numerous enough to meet what may suddenly become crying needs if the present trends in liturgy and religious education continue to grow. Those mostly involved in this evolution, therefore, are of necessity anxious to devise some quicker method of getting Scriptures in the vernacular than has been possible so far. More than once recently the idea has been aired of possible ways of co-operation with the "separated brethren". Church leaders have been approached unofficially; Bible Society Secretaries, locally and at headquarters, have also been contacted.

5. From several of the statements quoted in this booklet, it appears that the Roman Catholic view of the Bible, its place, its part in the total life of the Church, remains basically unchanged. Even if, in many ways, one can perhaps accept, with qualifications, or at least understand most of what is being said by Roman Catholic theologians about the necessity to read and study the Bible within the Church and her tradition if its full meaning is to be correctly apprehended and if full benefit is to be gained from it, there is, on the other hand, no sign of any general inclination on the part of Roman Catholics to recognize in the Scriptures the "cutting edge of evangelism". The Scripture for them—even in the form of a portion—is the Book of the Church: it is not for the outsider. Such a view cannot be shared by the Bible Societies. Their whole ethos is to make God's Word available to all men in their own language and to encourage them to read it, in the faith and conviction that the Holy Spirit, who teaches the Church how to interpret correctly that Word, is also able, beyond the fringe of the Church, to make God's Word persuasive and powerful unto salvation. The belief in the missionary power of God's Word is one of the

basic tenets of the Bible Societies. It is still not accepted by the Roman Catholics, even if—and this is progress—the educational, formative, transforming power of God's Word, within the Church, is being increasingly recognized.

6. This lasting and fundamental divergence, however, need in no way be an obstacle to any concerted efforts which might be devised and considered acceptable locally—see experiments in Holland, France, Cameroun—by Roman Catholics and Protestants to work on common translations of the Scriptures and to ensure their widest possible circulation and most effective use.

For such joint efforts there is a better climate today than ever before. And anyone who studies this development with a minimum of sympathy, or at least with an open mind, cannot but be led to wonder (if I may express in guarded terms what has become my deep conviction) whether we are not today confronted with one of those deep movements of the Spirit of God which seeks to revive and revitalize God's people, re-awakening in them the concern for the distribution and effective use of God's Word before it is too late! The Bible Societies and the other (Protestant) distribution agencies are just unable, by themselves, to cope with the challenge of the population and literacy explosions and of the spiritual threat of the modern world to the human soul. The Bible Societies have recognized the need of and the call for the fullest co-operation of the churches with which they are connected to increase the wider circulation of God's Word and its more effective use. The positive response on the part of many churches is undoubtedly a movement of the Spirit. We can only be deeply encouraged and praise God as we see that in the Roman Catholic Church, too, the Spirit seems to have initiated a convergent development.

> Behold, the days are coming, says the Lord God, when I will send a famine on the land . . . of hearing the words of the Lord.
>
> Amos 8:11 (R.S.V.)

1

Bible, Liturgy, and Mission

ROMAN CATHOLICISM has seen remarkable developments in its own life in recent decades. The biblical renewal has been paralleled by other most significant movements, such as a new outlook on and a new impetus given to lay apostolate, a revival of the patristic studies, the appearance of the priest-workers, the indigenization of the clergy and hierarchy in missionary areas, etc. Of particular significance in relation to the recovery of confidence in the Bible has been the liturgical renewal. Here the relationship between the two movements is more than parallelism. There is a deep interdependence between the two. In fact, the progress in the biblical field is inseparable from the liturgical revival and has received its impetus in large measure from fresh thinking on liturgy and its significance. This is particularly true of some of the most recent developments affecting the biblical movement in the Roman Catholic Church, and is mainly due to the fact that a new element has recently come into the picture and is giving a new dimension to the whole trend, namely the missionary concern.

For about a century, the liturgical movement had developed as the almost exclusive concern of small circles within the Roman Catholic Church, like the experiments in the Abbey of Solesmes in France, with Dom Gueranger, and more recently in other centres, like Klosterneuburg, near Vienna; Maria Laach, Beuren, Germany; St. John, U.S.A.; St. André les Bruges, Belgium; and various other monasteries and liturgical centres. In all these places the concern for a better use of the liturgy was linked with the concern for a more effective use of the Bible. This was underlined, for instance, in the title given by Fr. Dr. Pius Parsch of Klosterneuburg to their periodical launched in 1926—*Bibel und Liturgie*—a title taken up by periodicals representing a similar position in other languages. This complementary approach is also evident in periodicals such as *Revista Biblica* (Argentina), *Cultura Biblica* (Spain), *La Maison Dieu* (France), and in the recurrent interest shown by liturgical centres and in their publications in a richer and more meaningful use of the Bible in Roman Catholic piety.

> That Liturgy is nourished from the Bible had always been evident; but that the Bible itself received a new living power in the conduct of the Liturgy—*in media Ecclesia*—has only been recognized in our days. . . . The internal unity of Bible and Liturgy is *the* foundation of today's spiritual life.
>
> (X. Léon-Dufour, quoted in *Theologie der Gegenwart in Auswahl*, Verlag Gerhard Kaffke Bergen-Enkheim bei Frankfurt a.M., 1962, No. 1)

> This intimate relation between Scripture and liturgy was clearly brought out in the findings of the last congress of the "Centre de Pastorale Liturgique" (centre of liturgical studies for the clergy). The theme of the congress was Bible and Liturgy, "a choice which would have seemed perfectly incongruous ten years ago". The sub-titles alone are revealing: (1) No liturgy without the Bible; (2) The Church reads the Bible in the liturgical service; (3) The Church reads the whole Bible; (4) The whole Mass proclaims the Word of God; (5) Through the liturgy God speaks today; (6) The liturgy embodies today what the Bible proclaims; (7) The sacraments are biblical signs; (8) In spite of the increasing use of the missal it is with their ears that the faithful must listen to God's Word; (9) It is necessary that the faithful should understand the Word of God; (10) God has spoken in human language; (11) The Church responds to God through God's Word; (12) In the teaching of the faith to adolescents an effort is made to present the Bible through the liturgy; (13) The work of God's Word extends beyond the limits of the liturgical celebration. (*Bible et Vie Chrétienne*, No. 20, 1958, p. 117)

One of the main tenets of the liturgical movement today is to stress the necessity for any true renewal of piety and of church life, for a fuller participation of the people in the worship. In the course of the centuries Roman Catholic worship had increasingly become a celebration performed by the priest and his attendants, with only a very limited intelligent participation on the part of the congregation. The concern for liturgy emphasized the community character of Christian worship. God's Word needs an answer. The liturgy is precisely the ritual expression of this dialogue between God and His people, a dialogue which, incidentally, expresses itself in biblical language in the proclamation of God's Word and in the people's praise of the Lord, in their response, in gratitude, humility, repentance, and intercession, to God's Word and message to them.

> The aim of the liturgical movement is to bring the faithful to a more active participation in the liturgical life of the Church. . . . The primary reason for and the purpose of the liturgy is, without doubt, the worship of God. But the practice of this worship calls for the active participation of the Christian community . . .
>
> The liturgical movement aims at giving to the liturgy its true meaning: a corporate worship, in spirit and in truth, as well as a school of Christian spirit.
>
> (Cardinal V. Gracias, Archbishop of Bombay, in his opening address to the First International Week of Studies in Liturgy and Mission. *Missions et Liturgie*, Desclées de Brouwer, 1960, p. 31.)

But lay participation automatically raises the question of language. Thus, the problems of the intelligibility of the language of the liturgy had to be considered and necessarily, too, the question of the reading of Bible passages in the vernacular. This became a growing and soon a crucial problem as the liturgical movement emerged from its first period of somewhat esoterical and confused research and thinking.

Since the Council of Trent the use of vernacular languages in the liturgy has, for all practical purposes, not been possible. The Council itself had not expressly forbidden the use of the vernacular in the liturgy, but only stressed that "the essence of the Mass did not *demand* that it should be celebrated in the vernacular exclusively" (H. Schmidt, *Liturgie en langue vulgaire*, p. 52) as the Reformers had claimed. Nevertheless, the reserved attitude of the Council regarding the translation of the Bible into the vernacular and the emphasis put on the Vulgate as the official and authoritative text of the Bible made any development of the liturgy in the vernacular impossible. Even a French translation of the Missal was condemned in 1661 by Pope Alexander VII. For more than two centuries Latin was to be the language, and the only language, of the Roman liturgy all over the world, except in the Oriental churches attached to Rome, which had traditionally used the vernacular in their worship.

Timidly and almost incidentally, the question of the monopoly of Latin was raised in a Belgian periodical between the two world wars, and various liturgical centres started discussing the problem. Already at the beginning of the century Pius X had addressed an appeal for a greater and more active participation of the *laos* in the Mass, and this had given rise, eventually, to the publication of various private translations of the Missal; but it was, significantly, Pope Pius XII who, four years after his famous *Divino Afflante Spiritu* (which officially recognized the biblical movement and gave it its form), issued his Encyclical of November 1947, *Mediator Dei*, on the ministry of the Church and her clergy, in which one reads:

> The use of the Latin language, in a large part of the Church, is an obvious and unmistakable sign of unity and an effective protection against all corruption of the original doctrine. In a number of rites, however, the use of everyday language can be of great value to the people: but only the Holy See has the power to accord this concession; and without its knowledge and approval it is absolutely forbidden to do anything of this kind, for as We have said, the regulating of the Holy Liturgy is entirely dependent on its judgement and its will.

The same year Pius XII proclaimed the Indult authorizing the use of a bilingual Latin–French ritual, by which Latin remains the basic language; French is an auxiliary language. Moreover, the Holy See is the only authority to approve the translation, and any further alteration of the translation would necessitate a new Indult. All the same, this was a revolutionary step. Though occasional Indults, limited in space and time, had been granted locally by Bishops, in the case of the Indult referred to above Rome was for the first time extending the authorization to a whole linguistic area. Other similar Indults were later given, as for Belgian Congo and Ruanda Urundi (1956), Agra, India (1958), Japan (1958), Germany (1959). Indults have also been granted for various mission fields, sometimes experimentally or for special occasions. A bolder step was also taken in Germany in 1959 when, for the first time in the West, authorization was given to sing the Great Mass in German (*das Deutsche Hochamt*). Similar steps have been taken experimentally in various mission fields, where the Ordinary and even the Proprium of the Mass were allowed to be sung directly in the vernacular.

A first strong impetus in the direction of a general use of the vernacular in Scripture reading at the Mass came at the International Congress on Liturgy, Lugano 1953—though national liturgical congresses had already raised the question when discussing ways of implementing the recommendations of *Mediator Dei*. In Lugano Cardinal Lercaro, Bishop of Bologna, who also took a prominent part in the Vatican Council II, said in a paper given there:

> If the family of God in its liturgical assemblies could hear the Word of God in their own mother tongue, directly and immediately from the mouth of the minister empowered with authority to communicate it, the participation so much desired by the Holy Pontiff (Pius X) would seem to be more complete. He invited and succeeded in leading the faithful to participate in the liturgy of sacrifice by receiving the Eucharistic Bread; the direct use of the mother tongue for the Scripture readings would similarly enable them to take a more living and fruitful part in the liturgy of the Word of God by receiving the Word of God.

Three years later another International Liturgical Congress was held in Assisi and Rome. There the situation in the mission fields was taken into consideration, and the urgency of the need for a liturgical renewal there was proclaimed. One of the unanimous recommendations of that congress was "that people should be permitted not only to listen to God's Word in their own language, but also to answer in the sung Mass, by praying and singing in that same language".

Again, three years later, in September 1959, there was held in Nijmegen-Uden (Holland), as a follow-up of the Assisi

Congress, the first Week of Studies on Liturgy and Mission. It was conceived as a preliminary to regional meetings on liturgy to be held in all missionary areas, and was attended by thirty-seven missionary bishops, several other prelates, and heads of missionary orders, as well as some 100 priests, missionaries, or experts in liturgy or missiology.

The report of this conference makes striking reading in the recurring insistence it records, from all quarters, on the need for translations of the Bible in vernacular as the condition *sine qua non* of a real liturgical development and of a true implantation and rooting of Christianity in Africa and Asia. Missionary action, in the past centuries, placed the emphasis on schools and charitable institutions, bringing the benefits of Western education and welfare as an incentive to conversion. With the development of nationalism, the nationalization of schools and charitable institutions is proceeding rapidly. If not yet nationalized, these institutions are labelled as symbols and manifestations of Western imperialism.

> In concrete terms this means that in our missionary effort we must give priority to that which contributes the most directly to the achievement of these objectives. First and foremost comes religious instruction and the proclamation of the good news of the redemption, by spoken and written word, by sermons, catechisms and teaching by all possible media, including the press and radio, the employment of all effective means of announcing and preaching the Word of God, in particular through the liturgy. Then comes the incorporation of men in the mystical Body of Christ by the transmission of grace, supernatural and divine life.
>
> (Very Rev. Fr. J. Schütte, Superior General of the Society of the Divine Word)

Introducing the Reports, Fr. Parmananda Divarkar, S.J., also wrote:

> The urgency of the liturgical renewal in the missions asserts itself so obviously that the question which must have occurred to and challenged the members of the conference was: "How is it that the liturgical movement has made so little progress in the missions?" It has to be recognized that present-day missionary methods do not take

the liturgy sufficiently into account; and that, on the other hand, it was not possible either to integrate the liturgy into the present system nor simply to superimpose it. Such an undertaking would require more time and resources than the missioner has at his disposal: he himself has not received any liturgical training, he lacks competent aids, he does not even possess the necessary (reference) works such as translation of the Scriptures, or of chants in the language of the people among whom he is working, etc.

This echoes the statements made by most of the speakers.

It is not a privilege but a duty for the authorities to develop and improve the human side of the liturgy.

1. First general principle: the use of everyday language: to make the Mass comprehensible by using a language known by the congregation for the prayers and chants.

A "conscious and active participation" requires understanding, therefore a common language. This means: Bible, Missal, book of prayers and chants in everyday language.

(W. J. Duschak, S.V.D., Philippines)

While keeping for Latin the place which is its due, it seems to me necessary in the liturgy to increase the use of the living language. One loves to emphasize the value of the liturgy for religious education. But how can the Church teach the faithful if it has to make use of a language which they do not understand? The first preaching of the apostles was that of the day of Pentecost; but on that day all who heard them, coming from every part of the Roman world, cried with astonishment: "We do hear them speak in our tongues the wonderful works of God."

Personally I have a great admiration for the Latin language. But I maintain—*flens dico*—that we must certainly carry out a linguistic adaptation of our liturgical prayers if we wish them to remain live and vital.

(Emmanuel Larrain, Bishop of Talca, Chile)

We believe that Latin would have more value as the language for worship if those parts of the divine office which are in the nature of prayer and instruction were celebrated in a way that is comprehensible (to the worshippers) in the mother tongue and arranged in a dramatic form. In this way the people would be prepared for the act of sacrifice.

If then the priest carries out his ministry in Latin and stands before Christ like a mediator between God and men, this could make a strong impression.

(Fr. W. Bühlmann, Freiburg, Switzerland)

One of the essential foundations of all liturgical renewal is a good translation of the Holy Scripture into literary language.

(L. Nagae, Bishop of Urawa, Japan)

According to the biblical and patristic conception, the nations are only fully integrated into the "Peuple de Dieu" if they can praise and serve God in their own "tongue", in their own forms of worship. . . . No one any longer doubts that the training of the missionary must in future be based mainly on biblical, liturgical, and anthropological foundations. Through the understanding of the Bible we shall become closely acquainted with the religious sensitivity of the peoples of mission areas.

(Boniface Luykx)

Among the conclusions and findings of the Conference, one reads also:

The desire is expressed that the consecrated minister (or the celebrant) should be authorized to give the readings of the Mass solely in the language of the believers present, and turning towards them.

The number of Scripture passages read at the Sunday Masses should be increased, for example spreading them over a four-year cycle: in this way the treasures of the Holy Scriptures become more accessible to the faithful.

Since the liturgy depends on the Word of God, every encouragement should be given to the efforts being made to translate the Bible into living languages; and the faithful should be initiated in fruitful reading of the Scriptures.

(Report 6. Fr. Parmananda Divarkar, S.J., Bombay)

More recently the Rev. Fr. L. Mpongo, C.I.C.M., was writing in *Jeunes Eglises* (No. 5, 1960), a supplement for Africa to *Paroisse et Liturgie*, published in Elisabethville, Congo:

The early church did not choose these Greek and Latin languages through collusion with the lieu or culture of the colonizers, but because it was possible for the Bible to be translated quickly into these languages. It was, finally, the existence of a good version of the Bible which weighed the balance in favour of the living language which produced this translation, because the liturgy is too closely bound up with the Scripture.

The African languages likely to be used in the liturgy are those which will be able to prove their maturity through the existence of a valid version of the Scripture. . . .

Moreover, will not the role which the text of the Scripture will play then in the liturgy in one or other of our African languages, often be decisive in guaranteeing the maturity of this language and in preventing it from disappearing in the uniformist evolution of the present century?

The year before, at the Liturgical Conference held in Elisabethville (September 1959), Abbot E. Kilesbye stated:

I believe it is time to launch the Bible with all the precautions which are necessary. I think that if one showed the great plan of the history of God's people, not only once but many times, this would give a clear demonstration of the wonderful wholeness of the Bible. It only remains now to resolve the great question of translation, as well as that of putting the Bible on sale at a price which the ordinary man can pay.

Finally, the following quotation from a report published in the same periodical by Dom Thierry Maertens, of the Benedictine Abbey of St.-André les Bruges, shows how this whole movement and evolution lead at once to practical problems for the Protestant churches and the Bible Societies. Dom Thierry Maertens paid a long visit to Africa in 1959 in order to study the problem of liturgy in the African churches and to help them in their thinking and their action:

It seemed to me very clear that the most advanced Dioceses, in their pastoral use of the liturgy, were those which at the same time possessed a more or less complete translation of the Scripture. It is beyond question that a biblical text well rendered assures a greater religious maturity to the Christian population. It opens the door to a spiritually meaningful pre-mass service (where the Africans all too often still have to put up with hearing the readings in Latin!); it assures the possibility of the singing of inspired psalms; it brings the foundation of a profound renewal of the catechist and of the person receiving instruction.

One notices almost everywhere that the O.T. is particularly close to the soul of the African, even in certain turns of phrase. The plans for liturgical reform which consist of reducing the importance of the O.T. should be definitely opposed by the Church of Africa.

It is also necessary to emphasize the inadequacy of many "handbooks on the Bible", which summarize the accounts of the O.T. from a western spiritual outlook, omitting just those passages in the narrative which would please the Africans (dialogues, repartee, descriptive style, genealogies, etc.).

Young African priests who are disposed to study could become specialized in Hebrew and in the Scripture with a view to this work of translation. Only a few dioceses can already afford this luxury; others are faced with a state of linguistic upheaval such as makes any serious translation work unthinkable: furthermore the dioceses are often too poor to finance an edition of the Bible.

One solution envisaged is:

. . . the utilization of Protestant translations. With the agreement of several bishops I got into contact with the local Protestant authorities, generally more advanced than we are in the realm of Scripture editions. Each time they showed a great openness to the following propositions:

—the checking of the next edition with the Catholics, on the basis on the one hand of textual criticism and on the other of African linguistics.

—an optional edition, as an appendix, of the Apocryphal books.

—agreement in principle to the creation of an African Christian vocabulary (prayers, etc.).

—favourable reception to the principle of notes (many Protestants would accept notes of the order of those in the Jerusalem Bible).

I know that contacts are going on in the regions where I was able to have conversations of this kind. But it is too soon to forecast their results and to estimate their growth.

In the absence of a translation of the Bible, one could at least confine oneself to a translation of the Missal.

Turning then to the problem of the services of worship which, for the lack of priests, have to be led by lay-readers, Dom Maertens underlines the importance for them of satisfactory translation of the text of the Bible and of the Missal.

Let us return to the general problem of biblical translations. One of the tiresome things about the lack of translations is without doubt the poverty of inspiration at the prayer meetings with no priest. In many parishes praiseworthy efforts are made, but in the absence of a selection for Bible readings which would make possible a considerable deepening in doctrinal understanding, many of the villages have to restrict themselves to the repetition of prayers. In other places the cause of the difficulty is in the choice of (instructors) catechists who are often illiterate. Could not some solution be envisaged which would take into account present-day techniques? Every national radio system in Africa broadcasts the Mass. Could these broadcasts not be replaced, with advantage, by a programme aimed at these meetings without priests? It would be sufficient to make available to these catechists a radio set raised up so that the most backward villages could hear the voice of a priest speaking their language, reading the Scriptures in their dialect, inviting them to prayer—by the radio and to the chant given by the same programme . . .

A final comment regarding biblical translations. If it is true that the word of God must be made comprehensible to the African nevertheless this concern must not be exclusive. If the Bible is in human words, it is equally the supernatural Word. It can have its own vocabulary which one would betray if one wished to Africanize it to excess. There are plenty of biblical themes and images which have nothing African about them. Is one sure that one can paraphrase them with impunity? Should one not, on the contrary, initiate the African Christian in a biblical vocabulary and conduct? In any case it is in this sense that the Christian Latin of the Vulgate was built up (which is not the everyday Latin). It is in this general sense that a French Christian is in process of being trained, being under the direct influence of the vocabulary of the Bible.

The outcome of this tidal wave was the almost interminable debate at the Vatican Council, which in its first week prevented any further progress in the study and discussion of the first Schema proposed to the Fathers—the Schema on Liturgy.

The project, as far as available information would indicate, had embodied most of the theses developed in recent years by the liturgical movement. Soon, however, the debate moved from the generalities to the crucial alternative: Latin or vernacular tongues?

For the trend towards the use of the vernacular, as was made so evident in the earlier liturgical congresses, had not gone forward without a good deal of opposition on the part of certain circles in the Roman Catholic Church. In the Nijmegen congress the speakers themselves were careful to stress the need to maintain the use of Latin in some way or another, mainly on the grounds of the need to stress the unity of the Church, above the variety of languages. Some time earlier, the Cardinal Siri had written a pastoral letter on the burning question of the possible use of Italian in the liturgy in Italian churches. He was vigorously opposing the use of the vernacular and the maintenance of Latin, fearing that the use of the vernaculars would imply a complete revision of the liturgical texts, the need to adapt them constantly to changing situations, the suppression of most of the traditional texts, and the danger of erroneous interpretations of the revealed truths contained in the liturgical texts. God's worship is the supreme law of liturgy; this aim evidently transcends all pastoral advantages which the use of the vernacular may enhance. This attitude was shared by several high dignitaries of the Church, such as Cardinal Bacci, editor of *Latinitas* for the last ten years (a periodical which publishes only articles in Latin), or Cardinal Pizzardo of the Congregation of the Seminaries and Universities. The basic argument of all advocates of the use of Latin was the need to maintain and strengthen the unity of the Church, which could be endangered if, in order to satisfy nationalistic trends, the use of the vernacular were to be authorized.

A few months before the Council the supporters of Latin had marked a stage in the process, when the Apostolic Constitution of Pope John XXIII, *Veterum Sapientia*, February 22, 1962, was issued, encouraging the study and use of Latin in the Latin Church and prescribing that:

> Bishops and heads of religious orders should take care that none of those under their jurisdiction, urged on by a desire for novelty, should write against the use of the Latin language, either in teaching the highest of the sacred disciplines or in carrying out the sacred rites,

and that they should see that no-one, out of prejudice, should minimize or misinterpret the will of the Holy See in this way.

At the Council, however, in spite of a strenuous and prolonged effort on the part of the advocates of Latin to point out all the losses and potential dangers involved in abandoning Latin as the normal language of the liturgy, the pastoral approach, vigorously led by the representatives of the mission field, won the overwhelming majority of the votes, when, on November 14, the Fathers adopted the Schema *in globo* by some 2,160 votes against less than 50 and a few blank ballot papers: a "moral unanimity", as a Roman Catholic reporter put it.

Latin, it was now recognized, can no longer be the only vehicle of the liturgy and official prayer of the Church. Though maintained basically for the liturgy in the West, more room is left there too for the use of the vernacular, particularly for Scripture readings (which should be more numerous and more varied), prayers, and singing. The direct use of the vernacular in certain parts of the Mass and in the administration of Sacraments is now possible. It will be for the episcopal conferences at regional or national level, in consultation with the Vatican, to draw up appropriate plans and to work out the necessary adjustments.

"What falling to pieces there has been in this last fortnight; it is not only Latin: it is also the breaking up of a mental attitude," pointed out the reporter of *Informations Catholiques Internationales*.

2

The Bible in Religious Instruction

A FEW years ago (1954) a leader of the biblical movement, Father P. Démann, studied methodically all the available Roman Catholic catechetical literature in France—some 2,000 volumes: books for small children, manuals for students, textbooks for teachers, etc.

> A concern for this direct contact with the holy text [he states] has been—and still remains in large sections—almost completely absent from the teaching of religion. However, today we have an increasing number of pioneers whose opinion is more and more listened to, who have no hesitation in using carefully selected biblical passages as a basis for acquiring knowledge of God, and well-chosen biblical prayers—particularly from the Psalms—as a basis for the practice of a life of prayer. . . . Anthologies of biblical texts for biblical education are appearing in increasing numbers. The New Testament itself is placed more and more frequently in the hands of students, particularly in secondary schools. . . . At the end of such a study, one begins to wonder whether we do not err when we look for primarily sociological causes of the long process of de-christianization of which the fruits appear blatantly before our eyes today. "My people are destroyed for lack of knowledge" (Hos. 4:6) and "They shall wander . . . to seek the word of the Lord" (Amos 8:12). Today, timidly, a new hope arises: the signs of a catechetical renewal, inseparable from the biblical and liturgical renewals, manifest themselves increasingly day by day around us. The Spirit breathes in the Church, the same Spirit that speaks to us in the Scripture. (*Bible et Vie Chrétienne*, No. 5, 1954, pp. 196, 109.)

The following year another writer, Dom I. Fransen, reviewing the catechetical publications issued in 1954, confirmed the "evident desire to return to the sacred text itself".

Religious instruction and education is another key area of

Roman Catholic Church life in which the biblical movement has shown close interest. *Catéchèse*—the French term for this—is probably a more satisfactory expression, as it covers not only the religious education given to children and catechumens but also the religious instruction which men receive throughout their individual life and in the life of the parish, that is to say through the whole activity of the Church by which her members are helped to become better Christians, more *au fait* with Christian doctrine, history, and conduct, more fully equipped for their own Christian witness in and to the world. *Catéchèse* leads on into Christian service as the necessary complement of the liturgical preparation, which is the education and training of the members of the Church, as an outcome of having taken part together in the worship of the Church. Because of this we find a number of borderline cases where, as in the sermon, religious teaching penetrates the liturgy, or where, as in the many types of *ad hoc* liturgical "services" for schools and those young in the faith, liturgy becomes part of the religious educational process. Thus Christian education in its renewed perspectives is also tightly bound up with the tenets and developments of the liturgical revival.

The close link between religious education and the Scriptures has been put forward forcefully in an article published by the Benedictine Dom C. Charlier in 1956 in *Bible et Vie Chrétienne* (No. 12). He writes:

> Is it necessary to justify the present return to the Scriptures in catechetical teaching, when one thinks of the essential and unique place which the written Word of God has held for long centuries in the traditional methods of the Church? Everyone knows that the preparation, both long-term and short-term, of catechumens, consisted essentially in the reading of the Scripture, in commenting on it and in bringing fresh life to this reading, as to the commentaries, by introducing them within the living framework of the sacramental life. . . .
>
> Notwithstanding, for some centuries, especially since the Renaissance, this traditional method has been abandoned little by little. And today again the Bible takes practically no place in the teaching of

most catechisms, in the constituent churches as in missionary areas. Certain diocesan catechisms up to thirty years ago still required a lesson on the Scriptures—admittedly a very short one, since it only contained two or three answers to questions, of which one was practically warning against the reading of the Bible; but one learned at least of the existence of the inspired Book and of its nature as the Word of God. At present, if I am not mistaken, this lesson has disappeared from most catechisms, notably from the new catechism imposed for the whole of France; in vain one glances through it, but finds that the Scriptures, particularly the Old Testament, are practically not mentioned. The same absence is to be noticed in most manuals, at least prior to the last ten years; and what can be said of the oral commentaries which ordinarily accompany the rare allusions to the Bible? We have all heard said on such an occasion that the reading of the Bible was not to be recommended, that it was the battle book of the Protestants and that special permission was needed for opening it.

In the field of missionary activity a great biblical effort has certainly been attempted by certain special groups. . . . But can one believe that in missionary countries the Bible has experienced a progress comparable with that which it makes in Christendom, when one is obliged to acknowledge the disquieting silence which most missionary journals observe in relation to it, and the terrifying poverty of innumerable propaganda leaflets which so many missionary congregations distribute widely? The first task and the most urgent—as much for the missionary as for the catechist—is to become profoundly conscious again, intellectually of course, but equally so religiously, of the irresistible power of the Word of God. . . .

If the Bible is the Word of God, it is lack of faith to entertain any mistrust of it, as if the Holy Spirit, received with humility in the Church, could be anything but the source of all life for us. If the Bible is inspired by God, it is lack of faith to consider it as too difficult or hardly suitable to communicate the teaching of this faith. Yes, all our objections to the practical use of the Bible in the missionary and catechistic effort add up to a lack of faith. It is not a case of denying the difficulties, but as the proverb says, "where there's a will there's a way". Let us rather say, as Christians, "where there's faith there's a way", and above all when one believes in the Word of God. . . .

Before all else we have to become aware that if God has taken the trouble to speak to us, His Word is supremely effective, and it takes precedence over everything and is by right the fundamental source of all religious training. It is indeed the "handbook" of God.

Is this the same as saying that we must mingle the Bible and the catechism? Evidently not. The Bible as printed word is not the direct source of the faith. This faith the Christian receives from the Church. It is not therefore a question of substituting biblical teaching for the initial catechetical teaching. . . . The Bible is not the catechism but is its basis. It is not an organized framework of ideas. Its role is to give life to Christian education and upbringing, of which it is at the same time the source, the stimulus, and the expression. It is the source because the child or beginner must know from the beginning that the teaching of the priest or missionary is only a provisional adaptation of the Word of God itself, which is passed on to him through the Church in the Scripture and read in the traditional liturgy. It is a stimulus because a first initiation to the Bible, parallel to the dogmatic teaching, makes it possible to bring to life the teaching, by giving to it the irreplaceable value of a living contact, religious and supernatural, with the very words of God. And then it is the expression, because systematic teaching ought to give place progressively to the Word itself, by giving more and more place to the text of the Scripture, by bringing new life to the text through its use in the liturgy and by integrating it, like a sacrifice of praise, in the eucharistic sacrifice of the Word incarnate.

A first consequence of our renewed faith, which has been renewed in the inspiration of the Scriptures, should therefore be a revision of our methods, of our practical attitude in relation to the Bible, seen as an instrument of the catechism. . . . Every catechist, every missionary, should recognize anew that he is essentially committed by the Church to being the authorized trustee of the Word, "the witness of the message" and the reader of the Scriptures. . . .

Two recently published documents give us some indications of how this challenge is being currently met in Roman Catholic circles.

The most recent of the two is the July–August 1962 number of *Good Tidings—Aids for Teaching Religion*, published in the Philippines by the East Asian Pastoral Institute. Here is the editorial, under the title: "God's own 'Catechism' ".

Since its very beginning, some fifty years ago, the catechetical renewal has recommended the use of "God's own Catechism" in presenting His message. Modern catechesis is thoroughly biblical.

During the first period of this renewal, its pioneers emphasized above all the concrete and enticing way in which God Himself presented His message when He spoke to His beloved children.

The second period resulted in a new and unprecedented appreciation of the biblical message.

More so, it has discovered the Bible as a holy book by which we do not only learn about God but also are helped in a unique manner to come into personal contact with Him.

It has rediscovered that the Bible is the fundamental and classical Christian prayerbook.

It is the special purpose of this issue to show how the Bible leads an important role in the entire field of genuine catechesis, although it has to be used in quite different ways according to different age levels.

It will explain how the students have to be helped in their progressive approach to God's holy book: how they must not only learn to study but also to pray the Holy Bible, and how we can help them so that the Bible will become, in their early years and together with the Missal, *the book* of their very life.

The first article then expounds what the Bible is, namely, as the Editor wrote: a help "to lay the necessary foundations and to enkindle the right spirit of zeal and reverence with which the teaching of both the Old and the New Testament should be done".

The Bible is not *a* book about God, religion . . . it is "the Book".

It is God's *Word*—a *vivifying* Word.

It is God's *divinely inspired* Word which puts us in the *presence* of God as He *reveals Himself* to us, tells us about *ourselves* and our relationships with Himself, with our fellowmen, with the universe.

It is a Word telling us about God's *Thoughts, Intentions, Will.*

It is a Word expressing *God's salvific intervention in our history*; telling us about the *living, personal God as He approaches man* revealing Himself with a *masterful pedagogy;* manifesting Himself in *saving events.*

It is a Word that sets before us the "*Good News*"—the *Mystery of Christ*—the *plan of salvation history*, the course of the *economy of salvation.*

It is a Word which comes as a *personal invitation*, which we want to hear in the divinely inspired expressions of God; a Word which calls for a response on our part; a Word, then, which reveals *a dialogue* between God and man.

It is a Word which indicates that *this dialogue* is not a matter of past history, not an account of remote events, but of *one that continues today* in close continuity with previous events, in a certain re-actualization of those divine interventions—hence *placing us in the stream of salvation history*.

Various other main points follow: The Bible develops a strong sense of reality; it introduces its reader to a world of real people in vital personal relationship with God; it develops a sense of community, gives a sense of history and a sense of being in history. The article ends with the following comment and suggestions:

This biblical presentation can only be effective in catechesis when it is united with liturgy and a proper structural presentation of doctrine.

From the standpoint of teaching:

The Bible should not be looked upon as an accessory; not as a separate subject from catechesis, e.g. a course in Bible history; not regarded as a mine of stories, illustrations, text-proofs for doctrines; but rather as a departure for an integral, vital, dynamic presentation of revelation, as ultimately taught and interpreted for us by the Church. It is best taught in an environment that is sacred, by arousing proper dispositions for the hearing of God's Word. It calls for an apt selection of passages which present doctrine according to the pupil's present development and which set forth the moral demands of those caught up in this Christian economy of salvation.

A sample lesson follows, which, besides helping the children to detect and understand the various teachings of the story, continually refers back, not only to the biblical text being studied but also to other sections of the Bible, particularly the Psalms (thus establishing a link with liturgy and worship). The last part of the lesson is what is called "Celebration of the Word of God" and consists of three interwoven elements: brief explanations or "links" by the teacher, five short readings from the New Testament by five different readers, and a response by the class to each reading taken from Psalm 23 (The Lord is my Shepherd . . .).

The following passage is an extract from an article on "How to Use the Bible in Religion Class", by J. Hofinger, S.J., one of the world's most prominent promoters of the use of the Bible in religious education.

> Modern catechetics recommend great use of the Bible for all forms of the catechetical apostolate. The Bible deserves a prominent place in the proclamation of God's message, but many catechists betray in their teaching an almost insuperable reserve towards it. This is because they don't see how they ought to use it. Experience tells them that the problem will not be solved by merely increasing Bible readings during religion class. But how are they to make effective use of it?
>
> Some General Principles. Although the Bible has to be used in a quite different way with each age group, some general principles are valid throughout all grades.
>
> 1. We are gradually to lead pupils to the sacred text itself. According to Catholic understanding, God's written Word has the special character that not only the content, i.e. the ideas expressed in the sacred books, but also the manner of expression and presentation, is inspired by God.
>
> This is precisely the basic difference between God's own Word as we find it in the Bible and God's revealed doctrine as we find it in a solemn definition of the teaching Church.
>
> We therefore have to lead our students to the holy text itself. Genuine biblical catechesis means essentially more than telling Bible stories and familiarizing pupils with sacred history.
>
> To lead our pupils to the holy text itself does not mean that we should start with Bible reading at the very first year of religious instruction. We have to adapt our teaching to the age and level of our pupils. Sound initiation into the Bible must be progressive.
>
> 2. However highly we appreciate the catechetical value of the Bible, we never claim a monopoly for it. Bible catechesis is not and cannot be the only legitimate form of religious instruction. We fully accept and recommend other forms of catechesis, but they all need to be thoroughly imbued with God's Word to make up an organic unity with Bible catechesis. . . .
>
> In these first two years of religious instruction, we are preparing the hearts of the little ones for the later love and use of the Bible, and we do

this according to their age without using the book itself in religion class. It is not advisable even to show them the Bible in this early stage.

Reading from a big Bible in class would be the best way to turn them away from it, because books would not mean much, if anything, to them at this age. The best way for us to do is to use and keep the Bible at home, and go to the classroom with it in our hearts. . . .

But after a preliminary paraphrase we should use the very words of Christ, thus we develop in our pupils from their earliest years a holy reverence towards these life-bringing Words of Our Lord.

Let us in these early years make our pupils hungry for God's holy word . . .

In grade three it is time for the children to become acquainted with the Sacred Book itself. The Bible need not be a complete edition, but we deliberately choose the most beautiful edition at our disposal. The outward attractiveness of the book is important because at this age children are apt to judge books by their covers. We must also show them our appreciation of the content by having a Bible with worthy binding.

Even more important than the outward appearance of the Bible is our *whole manner of presenting it.* The way in which we hold the Holy Book in our hands must express deep reverence for it. The children, being naturally observant, will immediately notice our own reverence and easily learn from it a proper religious esteem for the Holy Bible. . . .

Henceforth, we should start Bible reading with our pupils. We would not give them a Bible nor even the New Testament, but the Bible should be given the prominent place it deserves in their text-book. . . .

Let us take care that the students *realize the reading of the biblical text as the climax of the individual lesson,* when the human teacher leads them to the Divine Teacher Himself who speaks to them in the Bible.

Besides the short passage from the Bible on the first page, the text of a pupil's book should provide, towards the end of each lesson, some well-adapted word from the Bible for memorization. . . .

About the age of ten or eleven the pupils are given the *privilege of reading aloud to the whole class the Bible passage to be studied.* This constitutes the first step towards a more advanced use of the Bible. The children should look upon it as a sacred service and a privilege. . . .

At this stage, the children's intellectual formation makes progress year by year. This fact allows and obliges us to *deepen our lessons from the Bible.* The pupils should now be able to understand the deeper meaning of the events and personalities of the Old Testament; they can now grasp the so-called types we find throughout the whole time of preparation for Christ and His work. . . .

For the first time, we must now go through a *whole book of the Bible.* This is an important step forward. A study of disconnected passages of the Bible cannot result in an understanding and appreciation of the Bible such as every educated Catholic ought to have.

For the Gospel according to St. Luke, we would need little inexpensive booklets of each of the four Gospels and the Acts of the Apostles. We do not recommend providing pupils at this age with a copy of the whole New Testament.

A good modern catechism is supposed to be thoroughly biblical and a modern catechist will teach the catechism with a thoroughly biblical approach. . . .

To attain this objective in high school we need to win our students to a *personal study and use of the Bible.* From the beginning of high school they ought to have their personal copy of the complete New Testament. They must have finished reading the whole book by the time they finish Grammar School.

Besides the passages we study and read together in class, we would encourage them to use this wonderful book for their prayerful readings at home. . . .

The biblical books, just like any other book, show the *individuality of the human author.* This the students will learn through their studies of literature.

They must be taught that God, when He spoke to us through human writers, did not suppress their individuality, but used them as His free human instruments; in a most admirable and divine adaptation, He availed Himself of their individuality as the means of a personal message.

The more our students become conscious of this human aspect of the Bible, the more we have, at the same time, *to develop in them a deep faith in the invisible and divine aspect of the Scriptures,* finding and acknowledging God by our faith behind and beneath the human appearances of His holy book.

The other articles of that issue include "A Biblical Prayer Meeting", a liturgical celebration "intended to offer to teachers of religion when gathered for a convention or a training course, a kind of spiritual recollection and meditation on their sublime vocation and tremendous task as catechists", and an article "How to read the Bible—a fundamental attitude" stressing their basic attitudes: "the Bible is the Word of God and should be read with faith"; "the Word of God has been written by men and as such it should be read with common sense"; the reading of the Bible also demands "a sense of history, a mature historical sense" in relation to God's progressive revelation of Himself.

The other important document is the third issue of *Catéchèse* (April 1961), a quarterly published under the auspices of the National Centre of Religious Education. It is almost wholly devoted to the report of the National Conference of Religious Teachers held in February 1961 on the theme: "The Bible in Religious Instruction", and attended by some 500 French teachers and visitors from some six other countries.

Some of the leading authorities in the biblical and religious educational field gave the main addresses, men like the Abbot Prof. P. Grelot of the Paris Catholic Institute and St. Sulpice Seminary, or Canon J. Colomb, P.S.S., author of a new catechism in which the Bible and biblical texts had a prominent place. (As a matter of fact, the first edition avoided being placed on the Index, only by the insertion of the last-minute "Errata" and "additions". A second edition was published in 1960 containing the necessary corrections.)

Professor Grelot's paper, entitled "Connaissance de la Bible" (Knowledge of the Bible), is an attempt to show some practical ways which current religious pedagogy could use in its present serious effort to integrate the Bible in the patterns of religious education. For many decades religious education and the Bible story remained largely disconnected. Today a considerable *rapprochement* has taken place: religious education is recognized as being devoted to the Word of God, even though it cannot just be limited to a commentary on Scriptural texts without any systematization.

The Bible is "functional literature", that is to say "adapted to the spiritual needs of God's people, as they were manifested in the centuries during which God's revelation took place. In this functional literature, each book, each section of a book, played a set part in the concrete presentation of the mystery of faith; its literary form has, of course, some relation to this object. . . ." Thus:

> Once we understand the diverse literary forms of the Bible, we shall understand what exactly was the part that the texts of which it is composed played in the life of God's people, both with regard to their general intention, and with regard to the literary forms that are used. And we shall also understand the part they can play today in religious instruction, an extension of their role in ancient times. In short, we shall be able to interpret them correctly.
>
> Every text has its natural place in our catechesis, corresponding to its original function and to its form.

The author then gives four main categories of texts: "Those which relate the history of salvation; those which deal with God's Law and wisdom for life; those which reproduce God's promises to His people; those which translate the prayer of God's people." But these categories correspond to a large extent to the main divisions of religious education. The task of the catechist, therefore, consists in using appropriate biblical texts and stories to give foundation to and to illustrate by concrete examples the dogmatic or systematic treatment of the material being studied. In this way, too, the student learns to read his Bible: having received a key to its understanding, he is more likely to want to go on with further reading, and he is better equipped for more meaningful apprehension of what he reads.

Even more immediately practical for catechists was the paper by Canon J. Colomb on "The Use of the Bible in Religious Instruction". He gives three pilot lessons of biblical religious instruction following a slightly different pattern: the historical approach, the aim and function of which is "to ensure, to bring to light the *objective, real, positive* character of the Word of God"; the theological approach, which is concerned with "underlining the *intelligibility* of the Word of God"; the liturgical approach, which has "to show the present relevance of the Word of God which continually challenges us during the course of the liturgy".

Here is how Canon Colomb describes the first approach:

We must choose the texts which are essential to religion, that is to say, the texts which express an essential aspect of the mystery of the faith. When we have chosen the text, we must bring to it the understanding which comes from faith. The explanations we give should not be in juxtaposition to the text; they simply bring out its meaning, and throw light on it.

This means that the essential aim of catechesis is to bring out the religious significance of the text. I want people to understand the Word of God, across the symbolism. Of course I take into account the human elements of the text: we should know and respect its particular literary form; we should place the events it relates in their geographical and historical setting; it is useful to notice what can be learned from it of the mentality of the Hebrew people. But in catechesis all this is necessary only in so far as it contributes to making the Word of God objective, concrete and living for those who are listening. Not only must we avoid laying so great an emphasis on these aspects, and from a point of view which is too exclusively scientific, so that we rob the text of its religious message; but further, even our explanations of the human data should guide the listeners towards a better understanding of the faith.

But if my reading of a historical event of the past is to lead to the understanding of a mystery and is to give rise to an act of faith, it is because this account, or rather, the mystery which it contains, *should appear to be of the present day*. The crossing of the Red Sea is a fact of the past, but the mystery it expresses is of the present.

It seems that this practical liaison is established easily by a presentation of the historic facts closely linked to the liturgical form of catechesis. What is evoked from the past is linked to the present in the preparation of the liturgical feast for the following Sunday, and still more in the actual celebration of liturgical feasts; in church there is the reading of the Epistle and Gospel, which relate events in the past but in the context of the community's action in the present, associated with the Offertory and the Communion, which are activities of the present. *The continuity of the liturgical act ensures therefore the continuity of past and present*. In this sense the crossing of the Red Sea is integrated into the general atmosphere of preparation at Christmas. It is not so much a part of history as a part of Advent.

The Canon's description of the second, the theological

approach, provides the opportunity of raising the problem of the relation between the Bible and Tradition, theology being based on an inextricable combination of both:

> Abbot Grelot has already given an answer to the problem of the relation between Scripture and Tradition, in drawing a distinction between the living Word and its crystallization in the written Word.
>
> Whether it is a question of the Old Testament or of the New, there is first of all the living Word of God, creating, illuminating, guiding, setting right the Jewish or Christian community, raising up the Prophets, Christ, and the Apostles. This mystery of the creating and illuminating Word of God in time expressed itself in writings; by the inspiration of the Spirit. Since then the Word of God has pride of place in the Scriptures.
>
> With the completion of the Scriptures and the death of the last eyewitness of Christ, "constitutive" tradition is completed. The Scriptures will no longer serve to *crystallize* what is the essential of the living Word, but will be a *rule* for the Church. The living Word cannot contradict the written Word; therefore, the written Word commands the attention of the Church. Nothing really new can now be added to the living Word, which Christ was, and which Scripture has established in its pages.
>
> The life of the Church goes on: a living community, knowing that it is under the command and judgement of the written Word of God, and also of the Spirit of Christ from within. The Scriptures and the Spirit are both within the Church, and the Church is in them. Both are for it a rule. Down the centuries, in the face of the new problems which the Church constantly meets, it reacts by referring to Scripture, to the light of the Spirit which the Scripture contains, and the Church's "experience" and growing "memory" continually add to the riches of the interpretation it gives to the written Word, in the light of the living Word.
>
> But there is a function of Scripture in catechesis which requires some emphasis. *The aim of catechesis* is not the possession of a formula, but *a living faith*, in a living relationship with the Trinity.
>
> Scripture draws my attention continually to this aim of catechesis. It confronts me continually with people who are speaking to me, challenging me and requiring me to answer in faith; it places me, not face to face with ideas, but face to face with Christ and with the Spirit. We know that even the words it uses, often symbolic, involve

all the breadth of our human nature. Throughout my talk I should be faithful to this direct, person-to-person attitude in which Scripture sets me.

Besides these introductory lectures, the conference was also sub-divided into six workshops where different aspects of the place and use of the Bible in religious education were examined:

Biblical Characters, as Witnesses of the Living God. (Describe the attitudes of biblical characters as the expression in one person of the very life of God's people, yesterday and today.)

Bible and Education in Prayer. (The Bible gives the true meaning of prayer. The Bible teaches us that all prayer is response to God and not human initiative. Regular contact with the Bible, Old and New Testament, initiates the child into the true meaning of prayer, which is an encounter with the living God, present and active. The Bible, from which we learn the true spirit of prayer, also provides us with phrases and hymns which the Church appropriates for her own use in the formulation of her prayer, following the example of Christ.)

Bible Stories in Religious Education. (It is very clear that a Bible story can be used fruitfully only if its specific literary form is respected. It is to be hoped that teachers of religion . . . will continue a true scholarly approach marked by a dual fidelity to the Bible and to the laws of religious education.)

Religious Education and the History of Salvation.

The Bible in the Catechetical Education of Adults. (Any catechist, when using a biblical fact, must relate it to the four stages of the history of salvation: the preparation in the Old Testament, the full realization in Jesus Christ, the working out of this plan for our benefit in the Church today, and its final fulfilment at Christ's return. The use of the Bible in religious teaching implies that the catechist should have in his mind . . . the great truths of the plan of salvation.)

The Place of the Bible in the Religious Education of Maladjusted Children.

Finally, the following general conclusions were adopted:

1. *Basically*

(*a*) Religious instruction must present the history of salvation revealed to us by the inspired writings of the Bible. (The Bible provides the whole of the mystery of salvation for our use in religious instruction.)

(*b*) Religious instruction must teach the mystery of Jesus Christ, which is at the heart of all scriptural revelation.

(*c*) In religious instruction the Bible must be read within the tradition of the Church. (The Church has been entrusted with the Scriptures. It is within the tradition of the Church that the Scripture is received and passed on.)

(*d*) In religious instruction the Bible is regarded as an ever-relevant message addressed to men today. (The Word of God contained in the Holy Books has in itself a power of grace and conversion. Thus, it is offered to men of all times and all nations, especially to those of our time in whom, by purification, it fulfils hope and desire by showing them the object of their hope, which is the salvation "*prepared by God for those who love Him*". 1 Cor. 2:9.)

2. *Rules and Principles of Instruction.*

(*a*) The teacher shall not see in biblical stories just anecdotes for illustrating doctrine. (It is necessary to present and explain the biblical story itself in such a way as to unfold the religious meaning of the Word God has intended for us.)

(*b*) The teacher shall take care not to present a succession of biblical facts like the unfolding of a story.

(*c*) In describing biblical characters, the teacher shall take care not only to bring out their spiritual qualities but also to show their relationship with the history of salvation, of which Christ is the centre.

(*d*) In his choice of stories and characters of the Bible the teacher shall take into account the basic plan of the course in religious instruction.

(*e*) The teacher shall proceed from the biblical fact to the mystery of faith. (Exposition in the religious instruction should respect the story as it is given in the Bible.)

(*f*) The teacher should favour direct contact with the holy Scriptures. (With adolescents one should create the taste for reading the Bible and help them to recognize the call addressed to them in God's Word.)

(*g*) The teacher shall take care to pass on the religious vocabulary which is indispensable for a knowledge of the mystery of salvation, and see that it is understood. (Personal preparation of the teacher.)

Finally, in the same volume, Abbot J. Péron, Professor in one of the seminaries, describes in some detail his experience with Bible circles for adults which are, as it were, the final stage in religious education:

> I have had the opportunity of using the "Bible Circle" method in several sessions in recent years: participation in a "mois sacerdotal", annual meetings with the team of diocesan workers, three- and five-day sessions with different groups of nuns (forty and sixty), seven-day sessions with the instruction teams (about thirty-five). I shall not record all that happened in these various sessions, but just describe the working of the Bible Circle, which was the basic unit. As the spiritual orientation is the same as that of the meetings I have already described, I will be a little more brief.
>
> Two subjects have been most frequently treated, in fairly long sessions: I Corinthians, St. Mark's Gospel to discover the pedagogy of Jesus. This year I think it will be the Revelation of St. John. . . . But let us turn to the actual structure of the circle. We will take as an example one day of the session of the Instruction Team. The circle met each morning from 9.30 to 12.30, dividing the time as follows:
>
> 9.30—10.00—presentation of the subject and formation of working groups.
> 10.00—11.00—research in teams.
> 11.00—12.30—plenary session.
>
> Let us consider each of these periods in detail.
>
> *Presentation and formation of teams.* The presentation of the subject by the leader must be very short. For this first session, it should include the necessary information for a general introduction: author, date, occasion, overall plan. It should include, too, a presentation of the section which will be the subject of the first circle: members should be enabled to grasp the structure and general progress of thought; thus they will have a view of the whole, before getting lost in the detail of

the questions set for each team. The essential element of this first period is the distribution of work to each team, inviting them to study carefully a certain part of the passage, following a set of definite questions. The benefit gained from the session depends very much on the way the work is divided up. The section of the text assigned to one team should be fairly short, and fairly complete. The questions should be few (four or five), very simple and clear. They should be fairly explicit, so that in replying to them the members find what is most important in the text; and yet they should make the members do real research work. It is not easy to get a balance between these two essentials. The questions chosen should lead to the spiritual content value of the passage, leaving aside more technical problems. The latter can be resolved by the leader, either in the presentation, or during the visit he makes at some time to the team he knows to be at grips with such problems.

Research in teams. The five teams, of seven or eight persons each, then disperse. It is important to see that the members move into their teams quickly, and go to the exact places assigned to them. A firm but pleasant discipline greatly adds to the success of such Bible Circles. This hour of work in teams should be used as follows: twenty minutes of strictly personal reading and research, forty minutes of discussion among the members and drawing up of conclusions. The team secretary (never the same person) should draw up a clear statement of the findings of the team and give a report on their behalf later on. Before breaking up, the team members are invited to pray about the Word of God they have encountered, and very often this prayer is coloured by specific intentions which have sprung out of the fraternal discussion.

Plenary session. The groups reassemble punctually, and the leader will see that the reporting time is divided fairly among the teams. . . . The secretary outlines briefly the answers found, mentions any difficulties encountered, divergences of interpretation or of spiritual outlook, and unsolved problems. The members of the other teams react in their turn. The leader himself speaks as little as possible, helps to make a point, comes to the rescue if necessary, guides the discussion back into the right direction, without communicating all his scriptural knowledge of a text. Thanks to the careful work of the team secretary, this pooling of conclusions can be done in an orderly but animated way. The time is always too short, and a rota is formed so that the same teams are not always given the chance to speak. This third AND

LAST PERIOD OF THE CIRCLE ENDS in prayer which takes up the points of the team prayers, or brings together several of the intentions proposed.

A "balance sheet". All experiments of this kind, whether with laymen, priests, or nuns, have been conclusive. Perhaps one loses a little on the precise didactical teaching which can be given in a lecture; one certainly gains in personal contact with the text, in the discovery on the part of the individual and of the group of the riches of the Word of God. The participants go away having acquired a taste for the Word of God and a certain technique for fruitful continuous reading. The normal result is a renewed Christian consciousness, sometimes even a real discovery of some vital fact of Christian spirituality which had been obliterated in routine presentation.

3

Progressives and Conservatives

POPE PIUS XII's Encyclical *Divino Afflante Spiritu* has generally and rightly been hailed as a landmark of the first importance in the recent history of the Roman Catholic Church. It opened the way for a modern approach to exegetical work, recognizing not only the necessity in matters of translation to go back beyond the Vulgate to the original Greek and Hebrew texts but also the need for a truly scientific exegesis:

> In the words and writings of the ancient Eastern authors, the literal sense was not as clearly evident as it is in the works of writers today; the meaning they intended their words to convey cannot be determined simply by rules of grammar or philology, nor simply by context. It is imperative that the exegete go back, as it were, in thought to these past centuries of the East, so that, with the help of all the resources of history, archaeology, ethnology and other sciences, he may discern and recognize what literary form these authors of old wanted to use and did use. . . . The exegete cannot determine *a priori* the forms of speech and expression used by these authors: he can only do it by a close study of the ancient writings of the East.

This was the outcome of a slow evolution started some half a century before and marked by *Providentissimus Deus* Encyclical, the creation of the Biblical Institute, the works of Fr. Lagrange, the well-known pioneer in the field of exegesis, the works of the Ecole Biblique of Jerusalem. Since 1943 this trend has gained in strength and width, and the market has been almost literally flooded with an abundance of Roman Catholic exegetical works of all kinds, many of which, according to expert opinion, are of highly significant value and have contributed towards bringing Roman Catholic exegesis at its best to the level of the most qualified non-Roman scholars.

Such an evolution could, however, not be expected to proceed without opposition from certain sections of the Church more attached to tradition and to the past. Even in moderate circles one has sometimes been wondering whether the exegetes in using to the full their newly won freedom were not undermining, unwittingly, some of the Roman Catholic dogmas by their exegetical work.

Pope Pius XII seems to have been alerted to this already when, seven years after his *Divino Afflante Spiritu*, he broadcast his other "biblical" Encyclical, *Humani Generis*. In this he stressed the necessity of maintaining the integrity of the Roman faith, and insisted on the need for strict control and sharp disciplinary measures on the part of the bishops and Church leaders over and against any misuse of the freedom previously given for biblical study—scholarly as well as within the Church's *laos*.

The strife between "liberals" and "integrists" within the Roman Catholic Church is not new. It has, however, taken a sharper turn in recent years, and various aspects of it have come to the attention of the public, as for instance in the matter of the worker-priest movement, or the use of Latin as indicated earlier in this booklet.

Similarly, in relation to the biblical movement, a growing tension has been manifesting itself in recent years, which came to an open conflict in 1960–61. One ought to be fully versed in all aspects of the developments inside the Roman Catholic Church if one is to be able to discern and assess the strength of the various components, theological as well as non-theological, which combine in a dispute of that kind. Besides a serious and genuine theological difficulty opposing the dogmatists to the exegetes (to which we shall return later), there were also the signs of an Italian opposition (integrist) to a "German" approach (liberal), of a cleavage or rivalry between the Lateran Pontifical University and the Pontifical Biblical Institute, and the unmistakable evidence of a concerted attack against the new exegetical movement.

The last phase in the conflict was the Schema on the Two Sources of Revelation, submitted to the Vatican Council II on November 14.

But let us look at the facts. At the end of 1960 *Divinitas*, a periodical edited by the Lateran Pontifical University, published a long and violent and, indeed, unfair article by Mgr. Antonino Romeo of the Sacred Congregation for Seminaries and Universities, which, as a Roman Catholic dogmatist put it, was "shameful and injurious to the honour of Catholic scholarship". This article attacked in particular two of the professors of the Pontifical Biblical Institute. Reprints of the seventy-page article were also circulated widely. An official answer was issued in the spring of 1961 by the Biblical Institute, protesting against what was considered to be a libellous action. The controversy led to numerous discussions in wide circles. On June 20, 1961, the Sacred Congregation of the Holy See issued the following Monitum, sent to the Roman Catholic bishops throughout the world:

> While recognizing a praiseworthy enthusiasm in the study of biblical sciences, there are judgements and opinions which are prevalent in various parts which greatly endanger the exact historical and objective truth of the Scripture, not only for the Old Testament, as Pope Pius XII deplored in his Encyclical *Humani Generis*, but also for the New Testament, even in relation to words and events in the life of Christ.
>
> Since these judgements and opinions have been the cause of some uneasiness on the part of the pastors and the faithful, the Most Eminent Fathers, guardians of the faith and practice, have decided to warn all those who deal with the Scriptures, whether verbally or in writing, for a subject of such great importance to do so always with the wisdom and respect desired. They are also urged always to have in mind the doctrine of the Fathers and the way of thinking and the majesty of the Church, so that the minds of the faithful may not be troubled and the truths of the faith not harmed.
>
> N.B. This Monitum is published with the agreement of the Most Eminent Fathers of the Biblical Commission. Given at Rome, from the Palais du St. Office. 20.6.61.

The postscript makes clear for whom the Monitum was mainly intended.

A few days later a *Life of Jesus*, by Albert Steinmann, one of the leading French-speaking "biblists" or biblical scholars, was put on the Index. Two months later the *Osservatore Romano* (August 24) published under the signature of Cardinal Ruffini of Palermo, one of the members of the Council of Chairmen of the Vatican Council, on its first page (where the "inspired" articles are generally to be found), another violent attack denouncing the undue influence over the Catholic exegetical movement of a group of "hypercritics" whose secret aim is to empty the Gospels of their real meaning by formulating false and misleading "working hypotheses". Indirectly the article seemed even to criticize the passage of the Encyclical *Divino Afflante Spiritu* quoted above, with its explicit commendation of the use of history, archaeology, ethnology, and other sciences in support of biblical exegesis. Cardinal Ruffini wrote:

> How can one suppose that, for nineteen centuries, the Church has presented the Divine Book to her sons without knowing the literary form which is the key to exact interpretations? Such an assertion becomes even more absurd when one bears in mind that a good number of the "hypercritics" not only put forward new methods of applying the theory of literary form to the inspired books, but expect to have final clarification only in the future, that is when more is known —through history, archaeology, ethnology and the other sciences— about the ways of speaking and writing of the ancients, especially the Orientals.

Another month, and another blow was launched in the *Palestro del Clero* in an article written by the Rev. F. Spadafora. Again the article was widely circulated in reprint form. Here various biblical scholars in France, Germany, and Italy were being criticized, but through them other leaders seem to be the real targets, as, for instance, the Secretary of the Pontifical Biblical Institute and possibly Cardinal Bea, the head of the Secretariat for the Ecumenical Council, and a former professor and rector of the Biblical Institute, who together had "stood surety" for the publication of an *Introduction to the Bible*, by Robert and Feuillet, a book which is the object of one of the attacks of the article.

A fortnight later the *Osservatore Romano* commented, after a lapse of one year, on the issue of *Divinitas*, the periodical which in 1960 had published the article of Mgr. Romeo, and this on the very day of the closing of the biblical conference held in relation to the celebration of the nineteen hundredth anniversary of St. Paul's arrival in Rome. It is also to be noted that no special papal audience was granted to the delegates to that conference, a fact which, apparently, received considerable attention in Roman Catholic circles.

Since then the debate has continued, though with less publicity; skirmishes were fought in the closed field of theological periodicals and reviews. But the controversy returned to the forefront at the Vatican Council II. A pamphlet by Prof. F. Spadafora—*Rationalism, Catholic Exegese, and Magistry*—again attacking the Biblical Institute, was circulated to all members of the Council. The Biblical Institute answered the charge by a short refutation. The stage was set for the debate on the theological Schema on the Two Sources of the Revelation introduced on November 14 by Cardinal Ottaviani. The document, which embodied most of the integrists' views, was widely attacked by most of the leading biblical scholars among the hierarchy and vehemently defended by the advocates of the traditional line of the Curia, the Cardinals Siri and Ruffini in particular. After four days of debate, Pope John XXIII ordered the withdrawal of the Schema and the preparation of another text by a mixed commission of the Theological Commission (Cardinal Ottaviani) and of the Secretariat for Unity (Cardinal Bea).

And now: what are the problems involved? A full and satisfactory analysis would need the mind and pen of a specialist. In broad terms, however, one can say, as indicated above, that the issue basically opposes exegetes and dogmatists. The latter fear that the work of the former is undertaken with excessive freedom, and may thereby undermine some basic dogmas of the faith and at any rate raise doubts in the minds of seminarists and future priests and through them and through the intelligentsia in certain sections at least of the *laos* of the Church. They accuse the exegetes of the Biblical Institute—rather by insinuation—of attempting to introduce into the Church the rationalistic criticism of Wellhausen's evolutionism and of the *Famgeschichte*. Fundamentally, it is the basis of modern hermeneutics which is being questioned: on the one hand, the exegetes claim the right to look at their problems without presupposed (dogmatic) ideas, but on the basis of objective principles derived from the laws of historical and literary exegesis itself. The systematic theologians, on the other hand, insist that the exegetes accept as a basis, and *a priori*, the principles adopted by the ecclesiastical authorities of true historicity and infallibility of the Scriptures. The argument of the exegetes then goes: the inspiration of the Scripture is a dogmatical fact with which they have no quarrel; the mode of inspiration is a theological problem, to deal with which is the object either of dogmatical treatises or of general introduction to the Holy Scripture but not of exegetical research. The answer of the dogmatist then points out that even if this is true in some measure, the exegete must not forget that he has to work within the Roman Catholic faith and to relate the results of his investigations to the recognized dogma of the Church.

There can be no doubt that the findings of the new exegetical research imply, if taken seriously, a searching re-examination of many affirmations and the necessity for certain theological problems to be formulated in new terms. The conservatives or integrists, however, fearing for the integrity of the ecclesiastical doctrine, insist on strict dogmatic and doctrinal delimitations which the exegetical studies should not be allowed to question, lest the faithful should be disturbed in their faith.

It is this approach which, according to reports, also underlay the theological Schema on the Two Sources of the Revelation, as prepared by the Theological Commission under the chairmanship of Cardinal Ottaviani in an attempt to ascertain anew and maintain unaltered the traditional Roman Catholic doctrine. One understands therefore the *mihi non placet* expressed by so many opponents on the first day of the debate: Cardinals Liénart (France), Bitter (U.S.A.), Frings (Germany), Alpink (Netherlands), Léger (Canada), König (Austria), Suenens (Belgium), Bea (Chairman of the Secretariat for Unity), to mention some of the most outspoken, and the decision to substitute another Schema, in the preparation of which the "biblicists" would also have their say.

According to an official news release, the Fathers who proposed the substitution of the Schema put forward the following motives: the excessively professorial and scholastic character of the Schema; its lack of pastoral emphasis; the fact that theological studies have not yet reached sufficient maturity; the danger of making truth incomprehensible to the separated brethren; the omission of the problem of the salvation of men prior to Revelation and of the non-baptized since; the insufficient encouragement given to scholarly research in the field of theology and exegesis.

The fate of the integrist Schema on the Two Sources of the Revelation (a title which in itself has also received wide criticism), following the acceptance of the progressive Schema on the Liturgy, is a good indication of the deep changes which the Roman Catholic Church is now undergoing. The biblical movement has certainly gained its rights of citizenship in the Roman Catholic Church and is exerting a strong influence in wide circles. The consequences of this situation can be considerable, both within the Roman Catholic Church and for its relationship with the other branches of Christianity. Within, the biblical movement has already made deep inroads in the fields of the Liturgy and of Christian education; soon dogmatic theology and ethics are bound to become involved. As for its ecumenical contacts, once more God's Word proves to be the sole meeting-place where Christ's disciples can meet in truth and charity and be one.

All the same, the conservative wing still holds to its position. In January 1963 details of a letter were prepared and sent to the Pope, signed by fourteen cardinals of the conservative group. In it the authors emphasized this concern with regard to certain trends evident at the Council, recalled the importance of tradition in relation to the divine revelation, and attacked four documents recently written by theologians related to the biblical movement.

On March 6, 1963, however, the Vatican Press Office announced that the new Schema taking the place of the one on the Two Sources of the Revelation had been completed and would be called The Schema on God's Revelation—a significant change. However, according to a recent interview with Cardinal Bea, it would appear that though unanimity had been found on all other points, no common view could be reached on the *main* one: the relationship between Scripture and Tradition.

4

Roman Catholic Translations in the Mission Fields

IN THE 1958 issue of the United Bible Societies' *Bulletin on the Bible and the Roman Catholic Church* reference was made to the fact that although a real rediscovery of the Bible was taking place in the Roman Catholic Church, there was no available evidence of this on the mission field. On the contrary, what documentation had been found on the subject rather tended to prove that the traditional attitude of discouraging the reading of the Scriptures was still the rule. (Previous chapters in the present booklet are a witness to trends which may lead to a considerable change in the situation.) This prompted the editor of the *Neue Zeitschrift für Missionswissenschaft* (*New Periodical of Missionary Science*)—a quarterly issued in Switzerland by the Schöneck Seminary (Beckenried) with articles mainly in French and German but occasionally in English—to publish a series of articles, as from the beginning of 1960, on the contributions of Roman Catholic missionaries in the field of Bible translation. At the beginning of 1963 articles were still appearing, though a good deal of the areas seemed by then to have been covered.

The series was opened by a long and thoughtful article by Fr. Dr. Walbert Bühlmann, O.F.M. Cap., a former missionary in the Swahili area and a specialist on missionary questions among the Franciscans. In this paper the author, like many of his collaborators in the series, refers with great appreciation to the achievements of the Bible Societies in the field and recognizes that the Roman Catholic missionaries have been terribly slow in setting themselves to the task of Scripture translation. Many different factors have, of course, contributed to this state of affairs: The Reformation and counter-Reformation; the Roman Catholic theology of the Bible; the Roman Catholic missionary approach, which starts more from the catechism (the teaching of the Church), biblical stories, and the Sunday pericopes of the Gospels and Epistles than from the Scripture, which is to be read within the Church and not used as a missionary tool. Such an outlook, however, has not prevented a considerable amount of translation work from being accomplished by Roman Catholic missionaries. Information about those activities, however, had never been systematically assembled, and it was the plan of the editor of the review to make such data available as a contribution to a more balanced appreciation of the small yet certainly not negligible contribution of the Roman Catholic Church in that field.

Finally, Fr. Bühlmann turns his attention to the problem of a possible co-operation between Protestants and Catholics in the field of Scripture translation. More and more the two groups have to face the same opponents—materialism, nationalism, resurgent religions, communism, etc.; more and more their scholars co-operate in biblical fields: archaeology, New Testament and Old Testament studies, and use the same basic tools, Kittel, Nestlé, etc. Why would it not be possible to extend such a collaboration in the field of the use of existing translations (for the mission field) or the joint preparation of new ones or of revisions?

In relation to the Roman Catholic practice in the mission field, the following paragraphs of Fr. Bühlmann's article are significant:

> The best form in which to learn the Word of God is the Liturgy—correctly composed! There one experiences the Word of God in the congregation, and it was originally and indeed is really directed to the congregation. There, as one follows with singing and with awe, one reflects on the Word of God in the Introitus, the Graduals, and in the Communion. In the Liturgy, in connexion with the eucharistic offering, one experiences ever anew the reality of the healing power of this Word. Whoever truly received the Word of God in the Liturgy—and in the mission area in many places there is still no Bible or translation of the Sunday Epistle or Gospel—already has a great deal, even when he did not engage in the private reading of the Bible. On the other hand, precisely through the Liturgy he is encouraged to draw more and more from the Scripture.

> But it still remains our belief that the Word of God was not given to the individual only but to the congregation, the Church, along with the individual.

The author then points to the dangers and indeed the disastrous consequences of a Scripture distribution assumed independently from the teaching and participation of the Church (multiplicity of the sects and heresies in Africa for instance) and to the need to protect the Scriptures from misinterpretation, this being the task of the Church, to whom, through the Holy Spirit, Christ has given the power of correct interpretation of His Word:

> In recent times the way has opened for some very encouraging developments which are leading to a convergence towards the centre of two extreme points of view. We Roman Catholics are . . . in the process of again giving a more significant place to the Bible in theology and in Christian life. At the same time there are the more recent statements that tradition does not represent a source of revelation *alongside* the Scripture; that the *totality* of the treasure of the faith has found its right expression in the Scripture and that Church tradition and catechetical teaching would have "only" the great task of continually making relevant for the day the apostolic tradition contained in the Scripture, that is to say, to place it in a living way in the setting of the present day, to explore current questions and give the answer to them, and ensure the right understanding. The Protestants, from their attitude of exclusive concern with the Scripture, are more and more reverting to the study of the Fathers and of tradition. They have definitely taken the lead today in patristic studies. The desire for tradition as well as for Church instruction will bring them to a concern for true theology. It may be, and is to be hoped, that we shall suddenly discover that here, too, as on the question of justification, we are not so far from one another as we think.

The series of articles themselves offer a fascinating collection of information and represent a considerable amount of historical and particularly bibliographical research. Most of them cover the developments in a given country or area, some in great bibliographical detail (Japan in particular), others with no indication of translators or publishers (India, in part at least). Two cover the activities of two of the most active orders in the field of translation at work in Africa, the White Fathers and the Fathers of the Holy Spirit (the latter also at work in the Philippines). The important part played by the Jesuits (Madagascar, China, Arabia, the Philippines, Rhodesia, India), the Franciscans (China, Japan, India, Ethiopia), the Order of the Sacred Heart (Oceania, Congo), also appears from the data given in the various articles. Also to be noted are the Salesians and the Foreign Missions (China, Japan, India), the Benedictines (Korea), the Carmelites (India).

But for a few exceptions (Chinese, Arabic, some Indian languages), it is only after 1850 that Roman Catholic missionaries seem to have developed some activity—if not in the translation at least in the publication of biblical texts in the vernacular. Here again, the main tongue has generally been chosen (Shona, for instance, for the Rhodesias, or Swahili) and the lesser languages neglected. This trend, however, is not apparent in the works of the White Fathers and the Fathers of the Holy Spirit or the Missionaries of the Sacred Heart. Yet it is from the article describing the activities of the Fathers of the Holy Spirit in Africa that the following extract is quoted, which, though not necessarily a reflection of the general trends in the Roman Catholic Church, nevertheless throws an interesting light on the situation:

> We would state that the joy our missionaries have had in the past twenty years in translating into the African languages has appreciably declined. And for good reasons. They do not want to work in something which has no substance.
>
> In the crucible which Africa is at the present time, the 650 languages, with their countless dialects, will of course be fused together. Swahili, or Kiswahili as we prefer to say, which is spoken in East Africa from the frontier of Ethiopia as far south as Rhodesia and to Eastern Congo, especially by Mohammedans, may escape, but the Christian populations of Uganda, Kenya and Tanganyika will speak English. Perhaps the 18 million Mohammedans in N. Nigeria will also keep their Hausa language, but in the Christian and government schools of S. Nigeria, as in the other former English colonies of W. Africa, all education will be conducted in English.

When the many new nations in the area of the former French colonial territories in Africa were created during the past year, the burning patriotism has nevertheless not led to any political action to declare one of the indigenous languages a lingua franca. They would have to get down to learning this language themselves.

This is the case with the poets and writers, of which Africa is so proud. Their work appears in English and French. Those who read them also read the Bible in English and French—all the young Christians. African Bibles have no future. Later they can serve as (historical) documents, to show the trouble which the missionaries have taken so that the people of Africa might receive their mother tongue and everything of value that goes with it.

In contrast to these rather drastic statements, here are the concluding lines of an article by a Jesuit Father writing on "The Holy Scriptures in Catholic India".

A great increase in Roman Catholic translations has taken place, especially during the past decade and following the second world war. The over-burdened state of many missionaries, the difficulty of finding adequate terminology in the various languages of India, the lack of education on the part of many Christians, the absence of suitable local resources and finally also the very uneven density of Christians in the individual languages, can certainly retard the work of translation, but does not prevent it from being undertaken. After the achievements of recent times, one may hope that the countless good attempts will be extended courageously.

In the first quotation from Fr. Bühlmann given above, one finds a perfect summary of the pattern generally followed in most Roman Catholic mission fields: first the catechism; then Bible stories; then the Gospel and Epistle readings for Sundays; then the Gospels, the Acts of the Apostles; then the Epistles and/or some books of the Old Testament, generally starting with the Psalms and the deutero-canonical books (the so-called Apocrypha).

Complete Bibles are very rare; complete New Testaments more frequent; but the late start in the field of translation, the slow development of biblical studies in the Roman Catholic Church, the diversity of the orders engaged in the work, the considerable degree of independence enjoyed by each missionary sending centre or monastery, the lack of funds no less than the pattern of translation programmes and the long-standing reluctance of Rome to give the biblical text "free", explain to a large degree the limited progress in the publication of Bibles and New Testaments. It is also symptomatic that with few exceptions (the Sicilian Franciscans in China and Japan, for instance, or the Salesians of Don Bosco in Japan), the Latin section of the Roman Catholic Church (France excluded) has not participated in the translation undertaking of the Church. The names of the translators are mainly German, French, and Dutch, unless they belong to nationals (Japan, China, Korea, India, Madagascar), who seem to have played a relatively important part as main translators.

With very few exceptions, the Vulgate or an existing Roman Catholic translation in a European language has served as a basis for the translations.

In conclusion, there are the languages in which translations have taken place according to the information supplied in the articles of the *Neue Zeitschrift* and a few additional data gathered elsewhere.

The whole Bible in Roman Catholic editions (sometimes with notes) exists in thirteen languages (Africa and Asia):

ANNAMESE (1913–16)
ARABIC (1671, 3 vol., Dominicans—Mosul 1878; Jesuits—Beirut 1880)
CEBUANO (Philippines, 1955)
CHINESE (1953, Franciscans, 11 vol.)
HINDI (O.T. in progress, N.T. published, Jesuits)
JAPANESE (Classical language: Franciscans, O.T. 1959, 4 vol. existing translation of N.T. No complete edition of whole Bible. Colloquial language: Salesians, N.T. published, O.T. in progress, first instalments, 1959)
KOREAN (N.T. published, O.T. in progress, first instalments 1958, Benedictines)
MALAGASI (1938, Jesuits)

MALAYALAM (1929, Alvaye Seminary)
NYANJA (Gospels and Acts 1936: Epistles and Apocalypse, 1954)
TAGALOG (Philippians, 1962)
TAMIL
URDU (O.T. 1924, N.T. already existing in other editions, whole Bible 1958 published in Rome)

The *New Testament* exists in thirteen additional languages. The following is a list of all New Testaments with the date of their first appearance; revisions and other versions have followed in many cases: (Africa and Asia.) Annamese (1913); Arabic (1650); Bemba—N. Rhodesia (1948–57); Cebuano—Philippines (1949); Chinese (1922); Ganda—Uganda (1953); Hindi (1958); Ilongo—Visaya (Panayan)—Philippines (1940); Japanese (classical 1910, colloquial 1953); Khasi—India; Kikuyu—Kenya (1955); Kirewe—Tanganyika (1946); Korean (1941); Lunda—Angola, Congo, N. Rhodesia (1963); Malagasi (1897); Malayalam—India (1930); Manyika—S. Rhodesia; Otetela—Congo (1946); Serer—Senegal (1927); Shona—Rhodesias (nearing completion); Sinhalese (1897); Swahili—East Africa (1956); Tagalog—Philippines (1953); Tamil (1953); Urdu (1864); Zezuru—S. Rhodesia; Zulu (1956).

In the following twenty-two languages only the *Four Gospels* or *Four Gospels* and *Acts* have been translated by Roman Catholic missionaries: Bengali; Bicol (Philippines); Bobo Fing (Haute Volta); Garo (India); Gunatuna (Rabaul—Oceania); Haya (Tanganyika); Ilocano (Philippines); Kabyle; Kurukh (India); Lingala (Congo); Mindo (Congo); Mundari (India); Nepali (India); Nyanja (Nyasaland); Oriya (India); Pangasinam (Philippines); Punjabi (India); Rundi (Ruanda-Urundi); Santali (India); Telugu (India); Tonga—Friendly Islands; Turkish.

Single *Portions* (mainly Gospels) have, in addition, been published in the following ten vernaculars: Bambara (Sudan Rep.); Ha (Tanganyika); Kalingga (Philippines); Kanarese (India); Kisumbwa (Tanganyika); Lugbara (Uganda); Luo (Kenya); Marathi (India); Sukuma (Tanganyika); Zinza (Tanganyika).

Finally, *Bible stories, Sunday pericopes* (Gospels and Epistles), *and other selections* have also been published:

French-speaking Africa	22	languages
English-speaking Africa	12	"
Congo, Ruanda–Urundi, Angola	8	"
Oceania—Rabaul Diocese	23	"
Various	4	"
a total of	69	"

Of course, Bible stories, Sunday pericopes, and other selections being generally the first publications to appear in a Roman Catholic mission field, such publications have also appeared, often in several different editions or translations, in nearly all the languages in which the Bible, the New Testament, or some books of the Scriptures have been printed.

As already pointed out, the above lists are not complete. There are, evidently, several areas where Roman Catholic missionaries are at work which have not yet answered the questionnaire of the *Neue Zeitschrift für Missionswissenschaft*. But the information already supplied certainly makes it possible to appreciate the relative importance of Roman Catholic Bible translation work, which, according to the available statistics, has covered 130 languages at present.

In another section of this book the statements of Dom Thierry Maertens have been quoted, in which he was evoking the possibility, in the field of translation, of Roman Catholic/Protestant co-operation. As a matter of fact, overtures have already been made to the Bible Societies in a few cases in India, Ceylon, and Africa, either for the use for Roman Catholic editions of Bible Society text, or for some kind of co-operation in the preparation of new translations or for revision work. Particularly significant is the following report received from Cameroun:

> We here in Cameroun are working on a joint Catholic-Protestant translation committee of Ewondo. A Protestant Cameroun pastor translated the entire New Testament and is presently working on the

Old Testament in Ewondo, or Beti. Through the initiative of the Bible Societies here we have been able to interest the Roman Catholics in co-operating in an endeavour to produce a translation whose text will be acceptable both to Protestants and Catholics. It is to be expected if we are able to produce a New Testament translation in this way that the text will be one text and the Catholics can add their imprimatur and footnotes as they see fit. However, because of the fact that the Ewendo population is almost entirely Catholic and because of the fact that there is some capable Protestant scholarship among the Ewondo, the Catholics are anxious that we co-operate with them in producing a text which will be entirely acceptable to Catholics and Protestants. So far meetings between the two groups have resulted in agreement on general orthography and the spelling of names and the like. I think for the most part this joint co-operation will be a revision of the present Ewondo New Testament rather than a new translation.

Finally, the same correspondent draws attention to a most significant development: the publication (in French) in Dakar of a journal for translators:

Another matter which I would suggest which is of considerable importance is a publication in French which comes from Dakar. Until the present this has appeared as a sort of an occasional bulletin and is entitled *Bulletin de Correspondances pour une Meilleure Traduction dans les Langues Africaines*. The address is Centre Culturel S. Dominque, B.P. 5098, Dakar. The name of the director is Père Grangette. This mimeographed bulletin is a sort of *Bible Translator* for French-speaking Catholics. Its purpose is to try and improve Scripture translations in African languages and it contains discussions of a linguistic and translational nature contributed by people all over French-speaking Africa. I have personal contact with a Monsieur Maurice Houis who is one of the directors of research at Ifan in Dakar and he is personally involved in this project. Recently when I spoke with him at Brazzaville and asked him about the continuation of the *Bulletin de Correspondances* he said that a new issue of some fifty pages has just come out and that he would be sending me a copy. I am looking forward to receiving it. The material contained in this bulletin is provided by individual contributors, most of them being Catholic missionaries, and there are discussions of linguistic terms in both the source languages as well as in African languages, and problems of translation. It is not of the quality of *The Bible Translator* but very obviously is attempting to pattern itself after this. I don't know exactly how wide a distribution it has and can't give you much other information on it. It has some excellent material and there has been some thought gone into the various articles that are appearing there. At any rate I would suggest that if you have still more time that you contact the above name and address to get specific and detailed information on this *Bulletin de Correspondances* which certainly will be increasing in importance in French-speaking Africa.

5

Facts and Events: Asia, Latin America, Africa, and Continental Europe

IN AN attempt to gather up-to-date information, a short questionnaire was sent out in the spring of 1962, asking for information about interesting developments which could be noted in recent times in relation to the place and use of the Bible in Roman Catholic circles. The following material has been taken from the answers received to which data gathered from other sources have been added so as to give as complete a picture as possible.

A geographical arrangement of the material seemed to be the most convenient. Developments in the U.S.A., however, have been reported in a separate chapter in view of the abundance of material and its particular significance.

Africa

Information has been received only from Madagascar, the Congo, Cameroun, East Africa, the Rhodesias, and English-speaking Equatorial West Africa. By and large, except for East Africa and the Rhodesias, there does not seem to be any particularly striking development in the areas covered. Although an increasing number of Roman Catholic Fathers and missionaries and some local clergy turn up at Bible Houses and show considerable interest in discovering the variety of Scriptures available, the reading of the Scriptures among the church members does not seem to have received much encouragement, nor to have been pursued systematically. Thus, in **Congo** only half of an edition of 10,000 copies of the Otetela New Testament (printed locally) has been sold fifteen years after its publication. (The Otetela number some 300,000 people.) The cost of the book being five times as high as the cost of the New Testament in a Bible Society edition may be a contributory factor to the slow sale of the books. Another, more recent, Roman Catholic edition of the Scriptures is a large volume of the Four Gospels in Lingala (imported from Belgium). Data on the size of the edition and the progress of the sales were not available.

A sign, however, of an increased interest in the Bible and concern for its use can be seen in the important Bible exhibition organized in December 1962 at the Roman Catholic Lovanium University. A number of Bible Society editions were also on display, as well as two of their posters encouraging the purchase and reading of the Scriptures.

A striking development took place early in 1962 in **Cameroun** (Duala), where a joint Protestant–Catholic Bible Week was organized, first in Duala, later in Yaoundé. In relation to the first one a correspondent reported:

> This took place in several ways. One way was the working out of a Bible contest which appeared in the Protestant and Catholic newspapers, and in the lay paper, and which was broadcast on a radio programme. The results were sent each to its own denominational origin, Protestant and Catholic, and the prizes were given by the Catholics to the Catholic contestants and by the Protestants to the Protestant contestants. We held also on two occasions in the Centre Culturel Français open discussions on the role of the Bible in Catholicism presented by the head of the Catholic Seminary and the equivalent from the point of view of the Bible in Protestantism presented by the Secretary of Churches and Missions in Cameroun. On another occasion we had an open meeting discussion on the future of African languages and the matter of translation in African languages in the country. In both of these there was full Catholic participation in the panels as well as in audience participation.

A similar programme was prepared for the Yaoundé week.

Information received from **Nigeria** indicates that there is no Roman Catholic vernacular translation of the Bible or of books of the Bible in existence, and it would seem as if "the possession or reading of the Bible as such is actively discouraged". "It is fairly evident that nothing is being attempted in Nigeria to stimulate the reading or distribution of Scriptures by the Roman Catholic Church," writes another correspondent. However, portions of the Gospel and of the Epistles (in English) are being used with students preparing for (religious) examinations.

In **East Africa** and **the Rhodesias**, on the other hand, certain sections at least of the Roman Catholic Church have come into the open, showing an evident concern for an effective use of the Bible in the life of their church, The Bible Houses in Salisbury as well as in Nairobi have been approached by representatives of the local dioceses with a view to finding out whether some co-operation would be possible in the use of the same or very similar translations in some languages, particularly Shona. Suggestions for co-operation in revision work were also made some while ago in relation to the Malagasy Bible, the Roman Catholic version of which is now being revised by a local team helped by French scholars.

As a matter of fact, the Roman Catholic translation of the New Testament in Shona is progressing, and the translators hope to have it published in 1964. They are attempting a kind of Union Version which should serve the three main Shona dialects: Zeguru, Manyika, and Karanga. (The first two already have a New Testament published by the Roman Catholic Church.) The editorship is in the hands of a missionary, Fr. Hannan, assisted by M. Gumbo, a member of the Shona people, who read Shona Literature at the University of Capetown. The editors work with a small translation committee on which all the three dialects are represented. The book will be produced on the missionary presses in Gwola.

Another interesting development was the free distribution in Tanganyika in 1961 of over 100,000 copies of the Four Gospels and Acts in Swahili, made possible by the gifts of two anonymous benefactors.

The biblical movement has a long way to go before the effective use of the Bible becomes a feature of Roman Catholicism on the Continent of Africa, and it is readily understandable that the wish for the use of Bible Society versions and/or co-operation with Protestant churches and the Bible Societies should have come mainly from Africa. However, pilot experiments have taken place in **Madagascar** in the diocese of Antsirabe, by which a better understanding of the Bible should be achieved. In 1959 a Bible Week was organized with a Bible exhibition. Catechists and lay preachers (who often lead services in the absence of the priests) had been invited to attend a biblical seminary (two lectures a day followed by discussion) which proved highly successful, according to a report (*Jeunes Eglises*, January 1960).

> If, at the beginning (the catechists) were not particularly keen on "wasting a whole week listening to palavers", they were all conquered by the Bible which they are now beginning to call "our Book". . . . To sum up, this Week of which we were all somewhat apprehensive, has surprised us all by the enthusiasm which it created among the participants and among the simple people who came to visit the exhibition or to attend our services of worship. This gives us cause to think. First of all, one must recognize that God is able to speak to His people at least as well as we can. And we have to take account of this in our pastoral work. . . . Our people also wish us to make an effort to make the Bible and any available biblical literature known. They even proposed the creation of an association with that aim. . . . They suggest, for instance, that in our visits we offer the Bible or publications about God's Word to sick people, to people in bereavement. . . . (With the exhibition) we certainly have a trump card, especially in a country where the Bible remains "the Book of the Protestants", a situation and a fact which our catechists in Faratsiho are not going to accept any more.

Asia

From evidence gathered—and, here again, it is far from being complete—one can fairly say that the Bible is given a somewhat more effective use in Roman Catholic circles in Asia than in Africa. Already from the previous chapter on Roman Catholic Bible translations in the mission field, it was clear that more had been achieved by Roman Catholic missionaries on that continent than in Africa. Nevertheless, it would be difficult to pretend that the biblical movement in Roman Catholic Asia has spread widely yet. Certain areas, like the **Philippines** and to some extent **India, Ceylon**, and **Hong Kong** show definite features of advance. But other areas are stalling, as, for instance, **Burma,** where there are no signs of any encouragement given to the reading of the Scriptures among Roman Catholics. **Japan,** though disclosing a considerable amount of work in the field of translation (the Franciscans are working on a new translation of the Old Testament), does not give any indication of an effort in the use and distribution of the Scriptures. Similarly in **Indonesia**, where rumours about a government grant to the Roman Catholic Church for the publication of Scriptures could not be confirmed. However, Scriptures have been ordered from the Indonesian Bible Society by Roman Catholics in slightly growing numbers in recent years, all indications being that these books were mainly intended for clergy and teachers.

In **Ceylon,** however, we find a comparatively large amount of biblical literature, summaries of the Old Testament and of the New Testament for primary classes in schools, as well as biblical stories in verse, and the still very popular Sunday Gospels with commentary written by the Rev. Fr. Jacome Gonselvesz in the second decade of the eighteenth century, the same priest having also written a remarkable compendium of the Bible, *Deva Veda Paranaya* (400 pages), in elegant Singhalese. The reading of the Scriptures, or at least of the Gospels, is occasionally encouraged in newspaper and magazine articles; in 1957 a Seminar on Bible Studies was held at Wannappuwa for Roman Catholic teachers, and a course of lectures on Bible aids to the teaching of the catechism took place last June for teachers and others under the patronage of the Archbishop of Colombo.

Up to 1958 considerable progress had taken place in **Indo-China.** This had been marked by an effort towards expository preaching, by the creation of study circles for young people (at which considerable attention was paid to the Bible), by the presentation of a travelling Bible exhibition, and by the publication of a considerable amount of religious material, including relatively large editions of Scriptures (in French): Four Gospels in one, 25,000 copies (1955); Mark's Gospel and Acts of the Apostles, each 10,000 copies (1956); Luke's Gospel, 5,000 copies

—because of paper shortage (1957); and thousands of copies of the Sermon on the Mount, Parables, Passion Story, etc. The partition of the country and the civil war put these efforts under considerable stress. However, the work seems to go on in South Vietnam. A Bible Week was held in 1961 in Dalat, including a Bible exhibition, the sale of Scriptures, lectures, and films on the Bible. A similar Week took place the following year in Saigon.

In **Hong Kong** and **Taiwan** (Formosa) a pocket edition of the Gospels (478 pages, HK$1·00—US$0·22) was published first in 1960 and again in 1961, each time in 30,000 copies. These publications were the first popular editions issued by Roman Catholic circles in Chinese. Other editions of a more scholarly nature, and supplemented with numerous notes, introductions, and comments, have been published in only 5,000 copies or even less (2,000, like the New Testament of Wu Ching-Hsiung (classical style) of the Catholic Truth Society, printed in 1960 (2nd edition), of which about half have been sold. The circulation of these Chinese editions, particularly the more expensive ones, meets with some difficulty, as a great part of potential Roman Catholic buyers prefer the Bible in English. At the same time, however, various efforts are being undertaken, particularly in Taiwan, to awaken more interest in Bible reading. Thus, plans are under consideration for the organization of Bible Weeks (essentially lectures about and on the Bible). In addition, a popular edition of the whole of the New Testament with short annotations was published in 1962, and at the same time a pocket edition of a biblical anthology has come out.

As for the **Philippines**, a "growing encouragement of the reading of the Bible, but only in English", is reported. This encouragement, however, is limited to Roman Catholic editions, and frequent warnings are issued against the use of "Protestant" "mutilated" Bibles.

In another chapter reference has been made to the special issue of *Good Tidings* on the Bible and its use in religious education. This is one clear evidence of the development of an active interest in the good use of the Bible. (See above, pp. 27 ff.)

Near East

In the Near East a few developments are reported, such as the circulation of a Roman Catholic translation of the Sermon on the Mount in Persian, a new translation of the Four Gospels and Acts in modern Turkish based on the Greek and published in 1959 in Italy. This last publication has not been circulated publicly, and the book has been given free of charge to almost anyone who asked for one. Illustrated Gospel stories have also been issued in Turkish by the Dominicans and are distributed to local parish priests for use with children.

The most significant development in the Near East recently has been the participation of Roman Catholic representatives at the United Bible Societies' conference in Jerusalem on the use of the Bible in the life of the churches. On the whole, Roman Catholic contributions to that conference were of an extremely high level. They did not reveal, however, any considerable effort in Scripture distribution or use in the congregation in general.

Latin America

Roman Catholics in **Argentina** are certainly the most active and progressive group in Latin America with respect to the use of the Bible and its encouragement. This is in great part due to the activities of the late Mgr. Dr. Juan Straubinger, a German scholar who took an important part in promoting the use of the Bible in Germany and Switzerland and was later (1937) moved to Argentina. There he himself initiated and worked on a new translation in Spanish.

One of the main tools of the biblical movement in Argentina has been the *Revista Biblica* (*Bible Review*) also founded by Mgr. Straubinger (1951), which combines articles on the Bible, exegesis, articles on the liturgy and its relation to God's Word, advice on how to read the Bible, general information on Bible Weeks and Scripture distribution and reading campaigns, and a considerable section of book reviews almost wholly devoted to books concerned with the Bible.

Two publishing houses, Herder and Guadalupe, both located in Buenos Aires, are engaged in Scripture publication. The most recent publication is a New Testament with plastic cover costing US$0·50, whereas cloth and leather cost respectively US$0·80 and US$2·50. In July 1962 Editorial Codex S.A., a commercial publishing house, started the publication in Spanish, for the whole of Spanish-speaking America, of a magazine-type Bible story (paraphrase) issued in weekly instalments and secured with full Imprimatur. Extensive radio, television, and press publicity was organized in relation to the launching of this periodical, as a part of an effort by the Roman Catholic Church in Argentina to get the Scriptures to the people. This undertaking follows closely the similar Italian publication by the publishing house Fratelli Fabri, S.L.R., Milan, which is also interested in the Latin America venture.

Scripture distribution also received a greater emphasis in Argentina than in other parts of Latin America. Thus, as Dr. I. Nothdurft points out in a report:

> In addition to regular sales in Herder and Guadalupe outlets, there are countless bookstores (Catholic and a few private) which serve for distribution of the Scriptures. Furthermore, campaigns for Bible distribution are organized. For example, a general summary of a programme of distribution by the Daughters of St. Paul is reported in *Revista Biblica* no. 96, 1960. They visited 57,433 families and distributed 21,210 books. Other details are given stating that 17 radio programmes were presented, 38 lectures, 37 illustrated talks, etc. In *Revista Biblica* no. 102, p. 208, a report is made by Padre Elias Clemente Dell'Oca, C.S.S.R., of a similar mission in the province of Corrientes. One could mention many of these missions which are being carried out in this area, including a description of methods employed (nuns going out two by two to organize Bible classes, sell materials etc.) In Uruguay we discovered that they were using our own materials (Gospel portions with a small religious picture pasted over the front) in their distribution work.

In the field of helps to readers, Editorial Guadalupe published an illustrated monthly magazine called *Reflector* for the Christian family. Suggestions are made in occasional articles. There is also a supply of catechetical material, which is, of course, interpretive of biblical material. Courses are presented to the public as reported in *Revista Biblica* no. 96, 1960, p. 64 and in no. 92, 1959, p. 105. The Department of Biblical Studies of the Institute of Higher Religious Culture organized Central Biblical Studies (*Revista Biblica* no. 90, 1958, p. 198).

Encouragement of Bible reading is the subject of innumerable reports which are made in this same journal. Bible Week is celebrated in the several provinces or states with all kinds of special conferences and messages. They also include dramatic productions of a similar nature to help attract the people to their public meetings.

One could point out public lectures being given in theatres. "Evangelical Conferences" are announced in bold letters on posters which give the idea that they are "Protestant" meetings. Farther down the name of the Rev. Padre will be given. Many of the methods and tactics which we have used through the years are being imitated.

Roman Catholic seminary students attended the Carnahan Lectures given in the Union Theological Seminary (Protestant) by Dr. G. Ernest Wright.

One can only report that there is a genuine and growing interest in biblical scholarship and divulgation in distribution in Argentina.

Regional efforts in Scripture distribution and biblical education are being organized all over the country in diocese after diocese. In August 1959 the Bishop of Nueve de Julio issued a pastoral letter encouraging the reading of the Scriptures in all his diocese and instituting the annual celebration of a Bible Sunday (the closest to September 30, the liturgical anniversary of St. Jerome) intended for encouraging "a better distribution and knowledge of the Holy Scriptures". The Catholic Action was also instructed to take steps towards the implementation of the appeal for a more effective use of the Bible, and 100 days of Indulgence were authorized for anyone reading daily a portion of the Scriptures. More recently, a booklet has been prepared and widely circulated—*Dios nos habla* (God speaks to us)—to encourage Bible reading and enlist members for this correspondence course in Bible study. The booklets are mainly distributed by nuns, who go out in house-to-house visitation.

It has recently been reported (*The Missionary Broadcaster*, August 1962) that a Roman Catholic Bible study group in Cordova, Argentina's second largest city, has started bi-weekly broadcasts over the most powerful local radio station under the title "Let's Read the Bible". The talks are on the book of Genesis. The Catholic publication *Didascalia* explains that the broadcasts were started "because of the great interest awakened by the many Bibles distributed recently through Protestant activities".

Considerable activity has also been shown in **Brazil** and, as the Rev. R. G. Nogueira, Bible Society regional secretary, points out:

> It is felt that the Roman Catholic Church is passing through a period of awakening interest in the Bible, not only on the part of the clergy but also of the general public.
>
> The old (Vulgate) translation by Fr. Antonio Pereira de Figueiredo in 1790 has just been re-edited by a secular publishing firm in various volumes and has been quite successful. Another publishing house brought out an illustrated edition of this same translation last year in a luxury type binding. In 1932, Fr. Mattos Soares from Porto, Portugal, made a new translation of the Vulgate which was printed in Brazil and has already reached its ninth edition in a popular edition.
>
> The Roman Catholic Church, however, has patronized other new translations. There is a group of translators working in Sao Paulo under the honorary direction of the Cardinal S. Mello Motta. This particular version is being made from the Hebraic text of the Old Testament by Kittel and the LXX text by Rahlfs and for the New Testament the text of Merck is being used. These translations are not being made by a team as they are generally done in our Bible Societies, but one or two books are given to individual specialists. Up to now, about one-fourth of the Bible has already been published in pamphlet form. It is an intellectual enterprise worthy of praise.
>
> The order of Benedictines has translated and edited a Bible based on the celebrated version of Maredsous. There are also numerous individual translations by regular and lay priests of the New Testament and separate books of the Bible.
>
> The Roman Catholic Church has patronized the Bible exhibitions and celebrated Bible Day on the Feast Day of St. Jerome. In the last Bible Contest promoted by the State of Israel, the Brazilian Organizing Committee included both pastors and priests.

A few years ago (1958) a considerable effort in distribution was undertaken in the valley of the Itajai, aiming at a Bible in every home, and similar undertakings are likely to have taken place elsewhere.

Reports from other countries, though all showing some signs of activity, are far less encouraging. Thus, only very recently the Archbishop of Sucre in **Bolivia** for the first time issued a Monitum urging the reading of the Scriptures, but no great publicity was given to it. Posters encouraging people to buy their Catholic Bible were also recently affixed in La Paz. Reports from **Peru** do not provide a very different picture, though there as elsewhere occasional Bible Weeks are taking place at which the importance of the reading of God's Word is being stressed by visiting preachers.

A report from **Mexico** (1961) referring to Roman Catholic and Protestant conversations mentioned the participation at them of the Bishop Sergio Mendez Arceo of Cuernavaca "who has been urging his people to engage in earnest study of the Scriptures [and] has been under attack by some Catholics because in remodelling his cathedral he did away with most images of the saints, replacing them with plaques bearing Bible quotations." (From the *Christian Century*, November 1, 1961, p. 1313.)

The following is also reported by the Rev. D. Lopez de Lara, Bible Society Secretary in Mexico:

> The Roman Catholic community during the whole year of 1961 organized, with notable success and great interest on the part of the participants, the "Movimiento Familiar Cristiono" (Christian Family Movement) which consists of groups of five married couples under the leadership of another married couple. They engage in the study of subjects such as the home, parent-child relationships, relationships among parents themselves. During 1962 these groups have been studying the Bible following the same methods as for other subjects.
>
> Occasional weeks are also being held in which lectures are given and special pronouncements issued encouraging the reading of the Bible. This year also, on September 30th, a national Bible Sunday was celebrated for the first time in the history of the Roman Catholic Church in Mexico, using every means of communication: religious press, secular press, radio, posters, etc. Bibles and New Testaments were offered absolutely free.

Again this year, a new translation in Spanish of the New Testament, based on the original Greek, was published by Colleccion Circulo Biblico de Toluca, Mexico. This translation was prepared by a group of scholars of the Centro Biblico Hispano Americano de Madrid. The book contains about 100 illustrations and, of course, many notes and commentaries. It is sold for Pesos 4 (US$ ·45) and 40,000 copies were printed.

The Roman Catholics are circulating a project to read the whole Bible except for the Book of Psalms and the Gospels. It is something like our daily Bible reading plans, except that they follow the religious calendar. This is a translation from the French, but Ediciones Benedictinas of Cuernavaca are doing the distribution.

Europe

Western Europe, along with North America, is the area of greatest advance in the use of the Bible among Roman Catholics. As already pointed out, in 1958 Austria, Germany, France, Belgium, Holland, and Switzerland were ahead of the Mediterranean or Eastern countries in this respect, the most evident sign of this being the almost incredible difficulty of getting reliable information or coming across satisfactory reports on the actual use of the Scriptures by Roman Catholics in these latter countries.

In **Spain**, however, two popular editions of Scripture have been published recently. One is a publication of the Four Gospels, translated from the original by P. Severiano del Paramo, published in Santander (2nd edition, 1960); the other a New Testament published by Herder in Barcelona but not translated from the original. Parallel with this the A.F.E.B.E. (Association for the Furtherance of Biblical Studies in Spain) has also put on the market a New Testament (4*s*. 9*d*. the cheapest), an edition of the Four Gospels, and a cheap abbreviated Synopsis considered as an introductory booklet to the further reading of the Scriptures. The same organization is also preparing an edition of the whole Bible. *Cultura Biblica* itself, the periodical issued by A.F.E.B.E., is devoted to encouragement of the reading of the Bible among the clergy and development of a biblical culture among educated laity.

The following information also recently appeared in *Frontier*, a British non-Roman Catholic quarterly (Autumn 1962):

> Finally, we must take note of a movement of true spiritual revival, peculiar to the Spanish Roman Catholic Church, which has been apparent particularly during the last ten or fifteen years. . . . The effects of the movement as regards Bible-reading have been excellent, in that study of the Scriptures has gradually come to play an important part in Spanish religious life. In 1944 the translation of Nacar Colunga appeared, and, in 1947, that of Bover Cantera. Since 1940 annual Bible Weeks have been held and since 1946 the Bible Day, which in some places has taken on a spectacular character, has been accompanied by large-scale publicity, including the distribution of numerous free or very cheap copies of the New Testament.
>
> We must also draw attention to the large number of articles, literary works and other publications on the subject of exegesis, criticism or biblical theology which have appeared since the Civil War, reaching in 1955 a total of 1,046 titles.
>
> The contemporary Spanish liturgical movement, with the use it makes of everyday language in worship, is an important factor in revival: the same may be said of congregational singing in church.

In **Portugal** there are also on the market various recent translations, single Gospels, Four Gospels, as well as a large-size illustrated New Testament translated from the original. There are, moreover, two handy editions of the whole Bible published by the Paulists and printed in Brazil. Bible lectures are also offered to the public by visiting preachers.

Little is being reported from **Italy**, except the launching by a Roman Catholic publisher in Milan of a Bible-story weekly magazine, parallel to the one published in Buenos Aires in Spanish. But the work of the Daughters of St. Paul, whose mother house is in Rome, is rendering a signal service to the cause of the Bible in the Roman Catholic Church through their publishing and printing houses in Rio de Janeiro, Buenos Aires, Madrid, Pasay (Philippines), Tokyo, and Boston, where a good deal of Scripture printing is taking place.

It would be too long and tedious to go over the whole range of publications and public activities which are intended for meeting the people's desire of knowledge, as well as for arousing that interest among churchgoers, in **France** and **Belgium**. Attention is therefore drawn only to some centres and groups particularly active in the biblical movement.

The "Ligue Catholique de l'Evangile" (founded in 1889), under the dynamic leadership of Fr. J. G. Gourbillon, O.P., continues its many-sided activities: its periodical, the quarterly *Cahiers de l'Evangile*, mainly devoted to the study of biblical themes or biblical books, and remarkably suited for a simple middle-class public as well as for the educated reader; its biblical competitions for seminary students; its service of Bible exhibitions and biblical lectures; its annual sessions of studies in biblical Hebrew, open to laity and attended by many Protestants as well as Catholics; its pilgrimages in the Holy Land, its circles of Christian culture, at which the Bible is being studied, as well as the main patristic and ecclesiastical documents, etc.

Bible et Terre Sainte is a fairly new periodical in which biblical archaeology, history, and geography hold a central place. Illustrations are abundant and fully educational. Each issue also contains some notes of "biblical news" and an appendix with practical suggestions for the adaptation and use of the material contained in the issue for Bible study circles, preaching, biblical talks, or religious instruction. Though archaeology, history, and biblical culture are the typical approach of this periodical, it is often a biblical theme (the meaning of the Resurrection, for instance) which is at the heart of the issue and which is illustrated. *Bible et Terre Sainte* also sponsors regular pilgrimages to the Holy Land.

Widely read also is *Bible et Vie Chrétienne*, published in France, but more closely related to the well-known Abbey of Maredsous in Belgium. Each issue contains commentaries on a biblical pericope or a biblical theme, as well as general articles appearing under the rubric of biblical and liturgical initiation.

Lumière et Vie and *Feu Nouveau* are two periodicals which also give considerable space to biblical studies. The main characteristic of the former is to examine first every theme it approaches—dogmatical or practical—in the light of the Old Testament and of the New Testament.

A report received from the Maredsous Abbey indicates that, so far, they have issued 220,000 complete Bibles, 183,000 New Testaments, and almost 2 million Portions. Their series of simple commentaries for less-educated Bible readers appear in editions of 5,000 copies each, but could reach a larger public if finances and time allowed for better publicity. Their Bible exhibition, more than five years old, is still shown in Belgium.

Among the new editions of the Holy Scriptures, the Jerusalem Bible and the Canon Osty New Testament are the best known, besides the Maredsous Bible and Bible de la Pléiade, a commercial undertaking (the Old Testament having been translated mainly by Prof. Dhormes, with one or two books by others, Protestant and Catholic, and the New Testament being in preparation by a team of scholars under the leadership of Prof. O. Cullmann).

Various popular editions of the Four Gospels in French have also been published in recent times, some notable for their various useful appendices: tables of miracles, characters, parables, evangelical themes classified according to catechetical, doctrinal, and spiritual categories (*Les Quatre Evangiles du Peuple Chrétien*, 382 pages, Editions du Cerf, NFr.1·80 = 2*s.* 7*d.* is the most remarkable). Others, like the latest edition of Maredsous, have aimed at an attractive presentation: chamois paper, sepia printing with green sub-titles and ornamental undulating rules.

A new venture also took place in France in 1962: the publication of a Gospel of Luke, under the title *La Bonne Nouvelle*, jointly prepared, including the notes, by Roman Catholics and Protestants. This booklet is intended mainly for home missionary distribution.

Every year a considerable number of new titles appear in the field of biblical literature: commentaries, exegetical works and studies, studies on the place of the Bible in relation to various aspects of the ministry of the Church, etc., all pointers to a continued and widespread interest in the Bible. Bible records are also eliciting considerable response, or so it would seem from their multiplicity.

Lastly, mention must be made of the series of biblical lectures which are organized in many dioceses, more or less systematically, and of the numerous Bible exhibitions organized locally (for which, incidentally, the co-operation of the Bible Society is sometimes requested, as in Florenville, Belgium, in 1961).

In view of the limited amount of information available, it may be more appropriate to refer here to the biblical movement in **Canada**, as it is found essentially in the French-speaking areas of the country. The Roman Catholic Church there is witnessing at the present time a very remarkable renewal, particularly in relation to lay movements. Cardinal P. E. Léger, Archbishop of Montreal, recently challenged the laity: "The layman, made a prophet by baptism, must become among his fellow-men a witness of divine truth. He doesn't preach in church, but all laymen, without exception, must become prophets of the Gospel in their own circles."

It is therefore not surprising that over 800,000 copies of a paperback New Testament in French, published in Quebec by the Association des Etudes Bibliques au Canada (their own version) should have been sold in the last ten years. It is a colloquial translation, and notes have been reduced to a minimum.

Without much publicity or strikingly new experiments, the Stuttgart Catholic Bible Work in **Germany**, and, in **Switzerland**, the Catholic Bible Movement (membership 1,600, almost exclusively clergy), both a quarter of a century old, continue their well-established and most useful service of encouraging Bible reading among the faithful by means of Bible-reading plans, with and without notes. Scriptures are being distributed free on various occasions and to various types of people. Bible Weeks are also organized in many parishes, and both organizations are able to supply audio-visual-aid materials for exhibitions, presentation of slides and pictures, etc. Clergy and religious teachers are also invited, at regional level, to attend biblical conferences at which methodical study of the Bible is taught and general biblical education given. Appropriate publications as background material for expository preaching are also issued and circulated in considerable numbers.

Besides these two organizations, Bible Weeks or seminars are also organized locally by various constituencies (Einsideln Monastery, for instance), again with the aim of preparing educationalists and priests to become better able to help the ordinary folk in the Church in their reading of the Scriptures. Notable from a scholarly point of view is the so-called Bible of Bonn—a translation and scientific commentary. *Bibel und Leben*, a quarterly published in Düsseldorf, also plays an active part in the biblical teaching of educated church members. The Bible Movement in Switzerland also published (1947) and circulated at nominal price an edition of the Four Gospels in Romansch (Surselvisch.)

A significant step was taken in 1960 by the Assembly of Bishops in Switzerland, when they issued a pastoral letter commending the reading of the Bible, encouraging the priests to give more prominence to the Bible in the liturgical life of their churches and requesting that in every church an open Bible should be placed as near the altar as possible so that the faithful may see that the Word and the Sacrament are complementary elements in the manifestation of God's presence. Church members were also encouraged to have in their homes, besides the Crucifix—the sign of atonement—the Holy Script in which they would find light and comfort.

On the other hand, in Germany the Catholic Youth Movement arranged, on Bekenntnistag (Day of Confession) 1961, a collection for the production of Scriptures in languages of Africa and Asia. A booklet containing the Lord's Prayer in several languages was on sale. Each young Catholic was encouraged to buy a copy, thus providing the necessary funds for the production of a cheap edition of the New Testament for overseas.

Mention must also be made of the scholarly work going on in the Beuron monastery (Benedictine) on the old Latin translation of the Bible, under the direction of Fr. Dr. Bonifatius Fischer, O.S.B. The whole compendium is to contain twenty-seven volumes, of which two or three have so far been completed.

Promotion of the effective use of the Bible and of its wider distribution has for nearly half a century been one of the main tasks of the monastery of Klosterneuburg in **Austria**. Fr. Pius Parsch opened the way and established this "Bibelapostolat". *Bibel und Liturgie* is their widely read periodical. But the monastery has also issued a considerable number of small publications, one of the best known being a booklet by Pius Parsch, *The Way I Hold Bible Study*.

The sale of Scriptures was encouraged for the first time at the end of 1961 by the use of promotional posters. In that year over a thousand Bibles and nearly 18,000 New Testaments had been distributed. So far more than 350,000 New Testaments have been circulated. The cheapest edition costs A.Sch.12—or 3*s*. 4*d*. The translation of Dr. J. Schäfer is being used for the New Testament. The text of the Old Testament (published in two volumes of over 1,000 pages each) is the work of a team of scholars.

The Bibelapostolat is also presently engaged, in co-operation with the Stuttgart Catholic Bible Work, in the preparation of a new translation of the Bible which, it is hoped, will be acceptable for the whole of the German-speaking world.

Like all similar movements, Klosterneuburg show a considerable activity in organizing Bible courses, Bible evenings, Bible exhibitions for clergy and for lay people. In 1961 and 1962 the Apostolate and the Bible Society co-operated in a Bible exhibition and lectures in three student-homes in Vienna. Some distribution work has also been undertaken jointly by youth connected with these two organizations. Symptomatic of the present outlook in Klosterneuburg is the following extract from a lecture given in the biblical "workshop" held at the monastery in the summer of 1959 by Dean Mgr. Dr. E. Hesse:

> What is the most profound reason for the Bible movement? The most profound reason is not that the Bible has something interesting to offer to us. Of course it has something interesting to offer, but that is not the determining reason that we would put forward. Even the Bible's ethos is not the determining factor. Indeed we know that this is not so easy to ascertain in the Bible, and that there are many problems there before we could really come to grips with it. Still more, it

is not because the faithful are in the position now of checking the teaching and dogma of the Church through the Bible. *Regula fidei proxima* remains the teaching of the Church and not the Bible. The Bible is the *Regula fidei remota.* That should be taken very seriously. Therefore with us it is still less—as it is with the sects—a case of using the Bible as a weapon against the Church. The most basic reason why we must bring the Bible to our faithful people with all our strength, is because Christ met with God in the dialogue. Christ is thus primarily a Christian-religious and not only in the general human sense religious, when he comes not merely praying, in a monologue, before God and the Eternal, but when He is truly engaged in intimate dialogue with God.

No report or information of any significance is available about developments in the Roman Church in Eastern Europe and in Scandinavia, except for news from **Poland** reported by the Catholic Press Service in Krakow in 1959 that over 1 million New Testaments in the Dabrowski version had been circulated in Poland since the end of the war. On the other hand, significant developments have taken place in **Holland** in recent years, where a Roman Catholic Bible Society was established in 1960 in Leiden and where a considerable amount of co-operation has developed between the "Protestant" Bible Society and the new Roman Catholic organization.

Simultaneously with the founding of the new Bible Society, a new Roman Catholic translation of the New Testament came off the press, a specially bound copy of which was presented to the Archbishop of Utrecht, Cardinal B. Alfrink. Copies were also offered to all the bishops in Holland. This gave them the opportunity of devoting their Lenten pastoral letter to the reading of the Scriptures. The bishops stated that their desire was that God's Word should be read daily and should more and more influence the believers in their personal, family, and social life. They also saw, in a more Bible-minded Church, an important contribution to a better understanding between Christians. "In the Bible and in listening to God's Word we find God and we find each other."

In the field of distribution, the Roman Catholic Bible Society joined forces with the Netherlands Bible Society on various occasions in sponsoring Scripture distribution campaigns undertaken with the help of Catholic and Protestant voluntary colporteurs. The first experiment of the kind took place in the autumn of 1960 in Laren; the Hague and Rotterdam followed. The following is a comment on the experiment, written by W. M. Abbott, S.J., which appeared in *America*, January 27, 1962:

> It has been instructive to watch developments that began in October, 1960, in the Netherlands. With the approval of the bishop, Catholic and Protestant volunteers, assisted by the Bible van of the Netherlands Bible Society, offered copies of the Bible from door to door in Laren, a city of about 10,000 people. They worked in teams of two, usually a Catholic and a Protestant together, throughout the day and into the evening. There was even a programme of "after care", addresses of those who showed interest were passed on to the various churches. The campaign began with a meeting at which both Catholic and Protestant clergy spoke. At a closing meeting there were expressions from both sides indicating appreciation of the common endeavour.
>
> In March, 1961, a similar campaign was conducted for four weeks in the Hague, with two vans of the Netherlands Bible Society operating in the streets. Catholic and Protestant teams went from door to door offering whole Bibles, New Testaments, and smaller portions of the Bible. Significant developments followed on a national scale.
>
> A fresh translation of the New Testament into Dutch had just been completed by Catholic scholars. A Catholic group was organized to distribute it. Faced with the technical problems of distribution the new group asked advice of the Netherlands Bible Society, which put at the disposal of the Catholics the experience it had garnered from 150 years of Bible production and distribution. The Netherlands Bible Society is on record with a statement that it is proud to have had "a genuine share in the technical planning of the new Catholic publication".
>
> The newly organized Catholic Bible Society and the Netherlands Bible Society then joined together in placing the Bible in the forefront of the national Book Week. Protestant and Catholic versions of the Bible were provided to bookshops everywhere for window display in various editions and at various prices. The two societies adopted the same slogan: "Book Week—Bible Week".
>
> Shortly afterwards, Dutch Catholics and Protestants joined forces

to produce two series of nationally televised programmes on the Bible, designed primarily for children. There were two cycles. The first, prepared by Protestant scholars, presented the story of King David from the Old Testament; the second, on the Resurrection, was done by Catholic scholars. The quality of scholarship involved is indicated by the participation of Dominican Father L. H. Grollenberg, internationally known and esteemed biblical scholar, who told a press conference before the first programme that modern techniques and biblical science are now bringing Catholics and Protestants together. He added, "The time when the Bible was a field of battle over orthodoxy between us is definitely over."

6

Roman Catholic Use of the Bible in the United States of America [1]

IT IS a curious anomaly that Catholics, popularly supposed neither to read the Bible nor to place too much reliance upon it, are nowadays practically the only people who continue in the calm belief that the Bible is the Word of God, and consequently absolutely true, although the official attitude of the Roman Catholic Church concerning the Bible is a puzzle to most people and needs clarification for all fair-minded Christians. In some Catholic publications the Bible is claimed as a Catholic book. The idea is propagated that it was the Catholic Church which held this treasure in trust for the world in its original and unaltered form. It is taught that the Bible is the infallible authority of the Catholic Church that always has been the only sure guarantee of its inspiration. However, the Bible itself is seldom read in the Catholic Church; there are no Bible classes in the Catholic Church, generally speaking, only occasional courses in Bible history.

The Bible—An Ecumenical Book

One of the chief differences between a Roman Catholic Bible and the Protestant Bible is not just the inclusion of the Apocrypha in the former, but also of the fact that there is not a single Catholic Bible that does not have notes. According to Dr. Eugene A. Nida, Secretary for Translations of the American Bible Society, as far as English Roman Catholic Bibles are concerned the best are Ronald Knox's translation based on the Vulgate (Sheed and Ward, New York, N.Y.) and the Confraternity translation (St. Anthony Guild Press, Paterson, N.J.). "It is unfortunate that in

[1] These notes were kindly supplied by the American Bible Society.

English the Roman Catholics have not put out a translation such as the French so-called 'Jerusalem Bible'."

According to the *Catholic Biblical Quarterly* (Vol. 23, No. 4, pp. 450–1), "If the announced English translation of the B.J. is published, the ordinary reader should be advised of the reason for the many discrepancies between this version (based on the Greek text) and the Book of Sirach as it is presented in the Confraternity Version (based on the Hebrew)."

Many Protestant and Roman Catholic clergymen have advocated that a unified Bible is a Christian unity step towards ecumenicism. A leading Roman Catholic biblical scholar declared here that one of the most effective steps in the Christian unity movement in the English-speaking world would be the preparation of a unified Bible acceptable to both Protestants and Catholics.

Father Robert A. Dyson, S.J., Professor of Sacred Scripture at Weston College, Weston, Mass., and formerly for twenty-nine years professor of Biblical exegesis at the Pontifical Biblical Institute in Rome, made a suggestion at a luncheon in his honour on January 27, 1959, attended by numerous Catholic and Protestant leaders. Noting that one of the purposes of the Ecumenical Council planned by Pope John XXIII is to discuss how best to "restore the unity we have lost", he said that "if we are going to work for unity, one of the vital things is to have all Christian denominations using the same Bible". He stressed that "a unified, scholarly, scientific presentation of the word of God that would be the best humanly possible is entirely feasible". Father Dyson said that only a comparatively few irreconcilable differences in Protestant and Catholic interpretations existed in either the Old or New Testaments, and this difficulty could be obviated by Protestants publishing the corresponding Catholic texts in footnotes, and vice versa.

He said he did not think "there is a single Protestant scholar who would not accept the idea of a unified Bible". And he pointed out that in France, Germany, and the Netherlands there are translations of the Bible taken from the original texts that are acceptable to all denominations.

The Episcopalian scholar, Dr. Dentan, told the C.B.A. (Catholic Biblical Association) meeting at Manhattanville College that he personally saw hope for a step towards ecumenicism in scholarly communication, and he emphasized the common interest in the Bible as a source of unity.

Some biblical scholars think that agreement in linguistic studies has reached the point where a uniform translation of the Bible acceptable to both Catholics and Protestants is a real possibility. Since Catholics and Protestants use the same critical editions of the biblical manuscripts as the basis for their work, it would seem an easy step to a joint translation of the Bible for the Christian people. The proposal of a common translation would eventually challenge us all, but especially Protestants, to reconsider the role and the location of the so-called Apocrypha, or deutero-canonical books. It could still more easily put an end to different numberings of the commandments, different numberings of the Psalms, and different spellings of biblical names.

There are interesting cases of objective co-operation in scholarship. The C.B.A. and the S.B.L.E. (Society of Biblical Literature and Exegesis) have agreed to exchange official delegates at their annual meetings from now on. The arrangement is some indication of the respect that Catholic and non-Catholic biblical scholars have for each other.

Father Bredan McGrath, O.S.B., President of the Catholic Biblical Association of America, declared in his address to the 1959 meeting of the Association that progress in Catholic biblical scholarship was due in no small measure to the altogether admirable willingness of Catholic scholars to avail themselves of the assured results and fruitful labours of non-Catholic colleagues.

Gatherings of Catholic, Protestant, and Jewish biblical scholars are not the rare events they used to be. Regional meetings of the Society of Biblical Literature and Exegesis bring scholars of all faiths together, and a feature of the annual meeting in New York last year was the session of the American Textual Criticism Seminar which presented a discussion of recent Old Testament text studies by Mgr. Patrick W. Skehan of the Catholic

University of America, and Professor Harry M. Orlinsky of the Hebrew Union College—Jewish Institute of Religion. Professor Bruce M. Metzger of Princeton Theological Seminary was in charge of the discussion.

Whether the R.S.V. (Revised Standard Version), adapted for Catholics, meets the needs, or whether some newly made translation would be required is a matter for further discussion. The fact is that the hope for a step towards ecumenicism in scholarly communication and the common interest in the Bible is a source of unity.

Towards a Common Bible

It is interesting to note that Christians are drawing closer together in their religious behaviour. The Roman Catholics are returning to the Bible. The Protestants are celebrating Holy Communion more frequently. In the field of theological study Protestant exegesis is becoming dogmatic and Catholic dogmatics are becoming exegetical.

A new joint translation of the Scriptures was begun by a team of Protestant, Roman Catholic, and Jewish scholars in 1960. Father Walter M. Abbott, S.J., editor of the National Jesuit Weekly *America* and one of the leading proponents of the "common Bible" idea, said the new translation will be published in thirty paperback volumes by Doubleday and Company, Inc. Heading the translation team is Dr. William F. Albright. Father Abbott said also that prominent Catholic and Protestant biblical scholars are in favour of a unified Bible as indispensable if Christian unity is ultimately to be achieved. He cited especially an endorsement by two Protestant scholars, Dr. Robert M. Grant and Dr. J. Coert Rylaarsdam of the Federated Theological Faculty of the University of Chicago. They said a common translation could exercise a unifying influence theologically and become a tremendous cultural force.

Father Abbott added that his proposal represents the first time that the idea of a common Bible has been published in detailed form for high church officials to study, and he expected much discussion and controversy. He said he expected it would take some years to achieve a unified Bible, because Catholic and Protestant churches in independent actions are at present engaged on new translations.

Two scholars, one a Protestant and the other a Roman Catholic, agreed here that there are some significant obstacles in the path of a development of a common Bible, even though there is general agreement on the accuracy of current translation. Dr. J. Carter Swaim, head of the National Council of Churches' Department of English Bible, cited the difference in theological interpretation of the passages which mention Mary. The Rev. Hubert Mckennie, S.J., from the department of religion at St. Louis University, said one of the main difficulties would centre around the different views regarding the Apocrypha. Dr. Swaim said that Protestants feel that in passages relating to Mary "the Roman Catholic translation is determined by theological presuppositions rather than by obvious meaning of original texts". Father Mckennie added that Catholics hold that the Apocrypha has a legitimate place in the Scripture, and any relegation to a seemingly secondary position would be offensive to Catholics.

(*N.B.* Following up in the same direction, Father Abbott also suggested, in 1960, the preparation of a "common biblical reader" intended for schools. The matter is still under consideration.)

Recent Publications of New Translations and Versions

The Catholic Biblical Association of America was formally founded in 1936. Preparation of a revised edition of the Challoner–Rheims Version of the New Testament began that year. The revised English text of the Catholic New Testament as planned in 1936 was published on May 18, 1941, known as the *Confraternity New Testament.* It has come into wide popular use.

A similar revision of the Challoner–Douay Old Testament was begun in 1938. In 1943, however, on the advice of the Pontifical Biblical Commission, and in keeping with the Encyclical *Divino Afflante Spiritu* on Sacred Scripture, this revision was abandoned in favour of an entirely new translation of the Bible made directly from the original Hebrew, Aramaic, and Greek texts.

On September 2, 1948, the Roman Catholic Church began

publication of a new English Translation of the Old Testament. It replaces the Douay Version for public reading in the United States. The Douay Version has been in use since 1609.

The Catholic Biblical Association of America supervised the translation under sponsorship of the Biblical Committee of the Confraternity of Christian Doctrine. A translation of the New Testament under similar auspices was first published in 1941.

The books of the Old Testament are being published by the St. Anthony Guild Press in Paterson, N.J., as was the Confraternity edition of the New Testament. The translation of Genesis was from the Massoretic Hebrew. Corrections that depart from this source are noted in a section entitled "Textual Notes".

Publication of two new versions for Catholics and Protestants (R.S.V.) was timed for the 500th Gutenberg Anniversary in 1952. Work for the Catholic version began in 1945 at the request of the American Roman Catholic Hierarchy, according to the Rev. Louis F. Hartman, General Secretary of the Catholic Biblical Association, Washington. He is chairman of the editorial board. This coincided with the publication of the Revised Standard Version.

Father Hartman said that the new Roman Catholic translation of the Bible would be in the living language of today and would be primarily the work of the American Catholic Hierarchy, who, acting through the Episcopal Committee of the Confraternity of Christian Doctrine, asked the Catholic Biblical Association of America to prepare this translation for them under their guidance and direction. The scholars who are translating the new Roman Catholic English Bible had the aid of Sister Emmanuel Collins, dean of the College St. Theresa, Winona, Wis., as a consultant on English style and usage.

Publication of the Mgr. Ronald A. Knox translation of the first half of the Old Testament was announced by Sheed and Ward, publishers, in 1952. Mgr. Knox was at work on the translation of the whole of the Bible for ten years. He made his translation from the Vulgate Latin of St. Jerome. He is recognized as one of the world's ablest translators of the Bible from the Latin Vulgate and Greek and Hebrew texts.

A Roman critic, J. Brennan, in *The Furrow* writes: "Whatever treasured phrases of the Douay Version are lost, the Bible yet benefits by Knox's reinterpretation and freshening up. No doubt Knox has sacrificed literalness, no doubt he phrases, yet he translates for the ordinary reader (not the scholar) for whom he must also be commentator." In other words, the Roman Catholic translator must interpret as well as translate, so that the meaning of the Bible may be conformed to the Roman dogma. The scholar knows better, but he holds that error must be used to keep the masses in conformity.

A unique Catholic Bible edition was published in Chicago in 1952, known as the *Papal Edition of the Catholic Bible*. The unique feature of the edition is that it incorporates, for the first time in any complete Catholic Bible, the latest Confraternity of Christian Doctrine translation of the Psalms from the original language. The Psalms have been published by the Confraternity, but only as a separate book.

A new translation of the New Testament into language "familiar to all who write and speak in the U.S." was issued by the Bruce Publishing Company in the U.S.A. in 1954. It is the work of two outstanding Roman Catholic scholars, Father James A. Kleist, S.J., and Father Joseph L. Lilly.[1]

Encouragement of the Reading of the Bible

Dr. James V. Claypool, former Secretary for the Encouragement of Bible Use, American Bible Society, stated that the Catholics have rediscovered the Bible, and continue to rediscover it day by day. Writing in the *Christian Life* Magazine (March 1952), he said:

> It is significant and provocative that in recent months Roman Catholic leaders are reproving their members for not reading the Bible more regularly and also identifying the Roman Church as the defender of God's written word.

[1]Bishop John J. Wright of Worcester noted that Catholics have published 264 editions of the Scriptures in English in America alone. More than fifty have appeared in the last ten years.

> The Supreme Council of the Knights of Columbus is engaged in a nation-wide advertising campaign which attempts to convince Protestants that the Bible is a Catholic Book . . . the Catholic Church highly esteems the Bible solely because God speaks to us through it.

> The widely read Catholic Weekly, *America*, used the occasion of World Bible Reading, sponsored by the American Bible Society, for a little more prodding of the faithful: The distribution of leaflets by the American Bible Society, announcing the opening of their annual Bible Reading Crusade, should remind Catholics anew of the treasures of Holy Writ which Holy Mother Church continually recommends for daily reading and meditation. To ignore Scripture is to ignore Christ.

In his article, "The New Turn", which appears in the *Zion's Herald Magazine* (March 19, 1952) he sums up the Catholic programme of the promotion of Bible use as follows:

> 1. Catholic leadership is zealous in its desire to bring afresh to its people the great resources of the Scripture itself for encouraging the love of God and holy and righteous living in this day.
>
> 2. Roman Catholic attitude toward the Bible is not nearly as narrow as Protestants ordinarily think.
>
> 3. It is important that this venerable ecclesiastical institution which we are wont to say "never passes up a good idea" and always knows a good thing when it sees it, is going all out for Bible reading at a time when Protestants are doing less Bible reading than their fathers and grandfathers.

The programme of popularizing the Sacred Scripture in the Catholic Press has been quite frequent. Editorials on Bible reading, feature articles on the books of the Bible, the use of Scripture in the explanation of Catholic doctrine, human-interest stories taken from the Bible, and the value of Scripture texts as fillers are appearing in numerous magazines and journals.

The Rev. John F. McConnell, Maryknoll Seminary, Glen Ellyn, Ill., spoke at the 35th annual conference of the Catholic Library Association in Chicago saying that an increase in Bible reading among Roman Catholics is noted: "a thirst for the word of God has become characteristic of the church's life". This new love of the Scriptures, he said, has gone hand in hand with a renewed appreciation of the Church's liturgy and a fresh vision of the Church as the mystical body of Christ.

The Rev. Gerald Ellard, S.J., of St. Mary's College, St. Mary, Kansas, proposed a change in the Roman Catholic liturgy which will substitute a two-, three-, or four-year cycle of biblical readings in the Epistles and Gospels of the Mass for the present one-year cycle. Such a change, he said, would aid the liturgy in giving fresh hearing to sacred Scripture by the simple expedient of having more, and at times also better, readings from Holy Writ embodied into the Mass and office.

A tremendous increase in Bible reading among Roman Catholics is discernible. This heightened interest in the Bible is widespread and intense. It is no fad, no mood of moment, no mere by-product of the popular interest in the Dead Sea Scrolls or the Gnostic manuscripts.

The Sacred Heart Hour Programme has twelve Bible Week radio programmes as follows: How to Read the Bible; Read the Bible for Faith; Read the Bible for Hope; Love Charity in the Bible; Read the Bible in Time of Sorrow; Read the Bible in Sickness; The Bible and the Sinner; Peace and the Bible; The Inspiration of the Bible; Story of the Bible; The Bible as a Rule of Faith; Catholics Use the Bible.

Many outstanding Roman Catholic biblical scholars and clergymen made a plea here for revival of the ancient custom of reading a portion of the Bible at every Mass until the entire Scriptures were covered during the course of the ecclesiastical year. The Rev. Agostino Bea, S.J., confessor to Pope Pius XII, speaking at the International Congress of Pastoral Liturgy, said that the custom of reading the entire Old and New Testaments in sections at Masses throughout the year had prevailed until the third century.

Bishop John J. Wright of Worcester made a plea to Roman Catholic priests and laymen to develop anew their love and knowledge of the Bible. The bishop cited the admonition of Pope Pius XII that it is the duty of the faithful to make free and holy use of this treasure. "The faithful must take up the Bible as we would a letter from Heaven addressed to each individually, to bring inspiration, instruction, correction, and courage." Bishop Wright paid tribute to the devotion of Protestants to the Bible, which resulted in a strong heritage of Scriptural moral idealism in Protestants.

At the fourth regional Congress of the Confraternity of Christian Doctrine the Rev. John E. Kelly of Washington, D.C., urged more direct use of the Bible in the teaching of Catholicism. Every adult should have his own copy of the New Testament, if not the entire Bible, and know how to use it.

Steps have also been taken at inter-confessional level. In February 1959 Catholics and Protestants observed a common Bible Week in St. Cloud, Minn. Copies of the Gospel according to St. John were distributed in every church. Associations of ministers, in co-operation with the American Bible Society, provided copies of either the King James (Authorized) Version or the Revised Standard Version. The Catholic Bishop of St. Cloud provided a special edition of the Confraternity of Christian Doctrine translation for Catholics. A reading for each day was listed on the front page of the St. Cloud *Daily Times*; Catholic and Protestant laymen spoke over local radio stations on what the Bible meant to them; priests and ministers gave biblical meditations over the radio in the morning; there were also biblical dramas in the evening.

One of the outcomes of the St. Cloud Bible Week was the publication in *Crosier Family Monthly* (March 1961), a Roman Catholic periodical published in Minnesota, of an article commending the practice of regular Bible reading in homes. Consecutive reading is recommended, followed by discussion (at which parents should listen and not only "preach") and by prayer said or read in turn by all the members of the family. Prefacing these practical recommendations, the author, Fr. F. X. Weiser, S.J., also wrote:

> When we read the Bible God Himself speaks to us. He talks through the words, language and style of a man; but everything which that man says is God's own word. With what joy and reverence should we then take these sacred books and devoutly read them! Even in the Old Testament, when many things were written for the Chosen People

of that time, you will find that God's word is timeless, given for our spiritual instruction at all ages, to the end of the world.

What is more, God not only talks to you. His very word contains the living power of grace: correction, warning, pleading, consolation, understanding and love. Our heavenly Father gave us these books for only *one* purpose: to reveal to us His justice, mercy and infinite love, in order to draw us close to Himself and help us attain eternal life.

In reading Holy Scripture, it is most important to keep in mind that the Old Testament and the New Testament are *one* unit of God's word. They belong together like dawn and daylight. The Old Testament contains the preparation towards our Redeemer. The New Testament is the "fulfillment", a glorious record of the divine answer to all the preparations, hopes and desires of the Old Testament.

Hence our Bible reading, also that of the Old Testament, must always be done with the humble and sincere attitude of looking how it leads towards Christ.

St. Patrick's Cathedral has been one high place where the reading of the Bible has been prominently encouraged on frequent occasions. Thus the Rev. Thomas A. Donnellan, who urged American Roman Catholics to cultivate a habit of reading the Bible daily, said the Church grants an indulgence of 300 days for anyone who reads the Bible in a serious manner for fifteen minutes every day; or the Rev. Francis X. Duffy, who declared that the Roman Catholic Church considered continual reading of the Bible so important that it granted plenary indulgences to persons in a state of grace who made Bible reading a daily habit. Reminding the congregation that Septuagesima Sunday marked the opening of National Catholic Bible Week, Father Duffy urged his hearers to "keep your Bible handy and read it every day".

Other Catholic clergymen urged their congregation that the observance of the Bible Sunday would help stimulate daily reading of the Bible by American Catholics. The divine inspiration of the Bible is a fundamental truth of the Catholic religion and the Roman Catholic Church has always held up the Bible to the faithful to be loved, venerated, and read.

Significant also is the activity of the Catholic Biblical Association. The following information is quoted from an article by a Paulist priest active in this organization, Father N. J. McEleney writing in *Eternity* (June 1962, p. 23):

In 1936 the Catholic Biblical Association of America came into being as the organization of scholars and others interested in furthering the knowledge of Holy Writ. Three years later the first issue of the *Catholic Biblical Quarterly* appeared. Since then, this magazine has won a place of first rank among the scholarly publications dealing with the Bible. On the popular level, there has been a steady stream of up-to-date Catholic works since the mid-fifties, beginning with such works as Father Vawter's *A Path Through Genesis* and Father McKenzie's *The Two-Edged Sword.* Among other publishing projects at the moment, two highly successful pamphlet series are commenting on the Bible. The Pamphlet Bible Series of the Paulist Press has begun its commentary with the Old Testament, while the Liturgical Press New Testament Reading Guide covers the New.

Classroom study of the Bible is increasing too. Each summer more institutions offer biblical programmes for sisters, brothers and priests who cannot get away from their teaching assignments during the year. Outstanding in this respect are the Catholic University of America in Washington, D.C., and St. Mary's College, Notre Dame, Ind. At the Maryknoll Seminary in Glen Ellyn, Ill., two shorter summer "institutes" on the Bible have brought together priests from all over the country. The number of adult education courses in Scripture is increasing. The Christian Family Movement has for its 1961–1962 Inquiry Programme the study of the Old Testament's relation to the New Testament and the liturgy. All of these things testify to the intense and intelligent effort being made by today's Catholic to develop his knowledge of the Bible's meaning.

By way of a parallel development in the field of piety, Bible vigils are gaining in popularity. The solemn procession with the Bible, the readings from the Scriptures and the commentary in explanation of them, the prayers and other acts of piety accompanying the Bible vigil tend to focus the Catholic's attention on the importance of the Bible to his life and worship. Though the Bible vigils have no set formula and are conducted differently in Baltimore, Boston, and Dallas, they have proved to be successful everywhere they have been tried.

One final result of the contemporary interest in the Scriptures deserves mention here. At no moment in history has there been as much good will and understanding between the adherents of different faiths as there is at present. The Bible offers an area in which this good will and understanding may be extended. Right now, scholars of all faiths and of none are co-operating in matters connected with biblical science, matters of textual criticism, archaeology, ancient history, and so on. For instance, Catholic priests and Protestant scholars are at work preparing the manuscript fragments from the Dead Sea area for scholarly publication. In Europe, Catholics and members of other religions jointly edit biblical periodicals. Such co-operation can only lead to a more charitable consideration of one's fellows as religious persons.

The Catholic Biblical Association has also taken an active part in furthering Catholic Bible Sunday, held annually since 1942 on Septuagesima Sunday and since 1951 extended into a Catholic Bible Week.

The most recent initiative of the Association has been the launching, in October 1962, of *The Bible Today*, "a periodical promoting popular appreciation of the Word of God", by the Liturgical Press, St. John's Abbey, Collegeville (Minnesota), starting with ten thousand subscribers. The aim is

> a publication that will provide a gradual and continuing education in the Bible for those who have not the time nor the background necessary to correlate all the published material. . . . Each article should leave the reader, not with some doubt about a traditional interpretation, but with a positive conviction about the meaning of the text or a clear impression of a biblical reality. (From the first editorial.)

7

Seen in Perspective

On October 14, 1960, the second year of his pontificate, Pope John XXIII conferred on the International Roman Catholic Biblical Society, through an official Brief, the name and rights of a "Unione Primaria", working under the auspices of the "Centre for the Preservation of the Faith" and under the general direction of the Sacred Congregation of the Council.

The scope of the International Roman Catholic Biblical Society is "the study, production, diffusion, and meditation of the Holy Bible, especially the Gospel, for the nourishing of Christian faith, morals and piety". "It takes its inspiration from devotion to Jesus—Master, Way, Truth, and Life." "The principal duty of its members is to pray that the Word of God, in the Bible, may reach all men, presented in assurance with the teaching of the Catholic Church."

The founder of the Society is the Pious Society of St. Paul, whose end is "to diffuse and augment Catholic life and doctrine by means of the press and other modern means".

The fruits and ultimate significance of this decision of the Pope have still to be seen. The proposed activities are multifarious, from the preparation and publication of Scripture editions to the promotion of biblical observances, the use of modern mass media in the service of the Word of God, the promotion of the practice of displaying the Holy Scriptures in a place of honour in churches, homes, institutions, schools, and associations, the promotion of the individual possession of a copy of the Bible or at least the Gospel, the furtherance of a greater and better knowledge of the Bible by means of study groups, lectures, correspondence courses, study days and weeks, literature, etc.

But more than the tremendous scope of these activities, which if implemented on a world-wide scale would result in the true return to the Bible of the Roman Church, it is, at this stage, the official recognition of such an undertaking which is symptomatic.

The facts and data referred to and assembled in this booklet cover only a short period. They are far from exhaustive. Even so, they offer a picture of the Roman Catholic Church which would certainly have been quite unthinkable only twenty-five years ago. The creation of an International Roman Catholic Biblical Society is another move in this relentless evolution which, since the end of the last century, has tended to bring the Bible back into the centre of the life of the Roman Catholic Church, and in the middle of which we find ourselves today.

The Encyclical of Pope Leo XIII, *Providentissimus Deus* (1893), was the first official manifestation of this recovery of confidence in the Bible. *Spiritus Paracletus* of Benedict XV (1920), and *Divino Afflante Spiritu* of Pius XII (1943), which celebrated the first jubilee of the biblical revival, each represented a milestone on the road.

The Vatican Council II now offers a new landmark. Its first session has ended on a formal draw between the biblicists and the integrists. Seen in perspective, however, this draw gives the measure of the immense gains made by the biblical movement in the last half-century.

What the future holds in store no one, of course, can tell. But, because we see in this evolution one aspect of the deep action of God's Spirit in the whole Christian Church today—Protestant as well as Orthodox or Roman Catholic—preparing her to meet the challenge of the "new age", we can be of good cheer: the Bible will also be heard in Rome tomorrow, as it is already today.